D0927163

How Pasteur Changed History

The story of Louis Pasteur and the Pasteur Institute

Moira Davison Reynolds

McGuinn & McGuire
PUBLISHING, INC
Bradenton, Florida

How Pasteur Changed History. Copyright 1994 by Moira Davison Reynolds. Printed and bound in the United States of America. All rights reserved. No part of this book may be reproduced or transmitted in any form or by any means, electronic or mechanical, including photocopying, recording, or by any information storage or retrieval system without permission in writing from the publisher, except by a reviewer who may quote brief passages in a review to be printed in a magazine or newspaper. For information, contact McGuinn & McGuire Publishing, Inc., Post Office Box 20603, Bradenton, Florida 34203.

Library of Congress Cataloging-in-Publication Data

Reynolds, Moira Davison.
    How Pasteur Changed History: the story of Louis Pasteur and the
Pasteur Insitute / Moira Davison Reynolds
        p.   cm.
    Includes bibliographical references and index.
    ISBN 1-881117-05-7 (pbk.)
    1. Pasteur, Louis, 1822-1895. 2. Institut Pasteur (Paris, France)—
History. 3. Science—History. 4. Medical sciences—France—History.
Scientist—France—Biography. I. Title.
Q143.P2R49 1994
509.2—dc20
[B]   94-2757
                                                               CIP

Printed in the United States of America

To Avery Asa Reynolds,
dearly loved grandchild.

ACKNOWLEDGMENTS

Louis Pasteur is an unusual figure whose like will probably not be seen again. His inspirational story has fascinated me for many years. I hope I have presented it in a form appealing to the reader who is a nonscientist.

I have gleaned the details of Pasteur's life from several sources, especially the Vallery-Radot biography, written some time ago by his son-in-law. I am indebted to many for help with this project: Mildred Kingsbury and Theresa Scram of the staff of the Kevin F. O'Brien Health Sciences Library, Marquette General Hospital; the staffs of Peter White Public Library, Marquette, and of Lydia M. Olson Library, Northern Michigan University. My long-standing mainstay, Joanne Whitley of Superiorland Library Cooperative, deserves special mention. A. Labastire of the Pasteur Institute furnished me with abundant material, as did Caitlin Hawke of the Pasteur Foundation, New York City. My thanks to the American Cancer Society for supplying diagrams and to Mary Frey of Lake Superior Press for line drawings. A special thank you to Orland Reynolds, my husband, for his critical reading of the manuscript and to Ronald Reynolds, M.D., our son, for checking certain medical facts. Finally, I wish to express my appreciation to Christopher Carroll, Managing Editor at McGuinn & McGuire Publishing, for helpful suggestions.

Moira Davison Reynolds
Marquette, Michigan

CONTENTS

That which puts him outside of comparison is the fact that he loved great horizons, knew how to discover them and to make himself a part of them.

Emile Duclaux

Chapter 1

PRELUDE

March, 1879 – Of every 19 women who entered the maternity hospitals of Paris, one died. As a member of the Academy of Medicine was orating about his theory on the deadly epidemics, he was interrupted by another member.

"It is nothing of the kind! It is the doctor and his staff who carry the microorganism from a sick to a healthy woman."

The first speaker answered he feared that microbe would never be found.

The second speaker left his seat, limping to the blackboard. He drew a chain of small circles. "There!" he cried impatiently, "There is its picture!" His iron-gray hair and his tone gave him an air of authority.

The man who came forward was Louis Pasteur. This is the story of how his contributions to science changed history.

Louis Pasteur was born on December 27, 1822, in Dôle, a French village some 60 miles west of the Swiss border.

The year had seen the birth of Gregor Mendel, another scientist who would attain lasting fame; the world had been given Schubert's Unfinished Symphony; in France, Louis XVIII sat on the throne. In the United States, James Madison was president, and the streets of Boston had recently been lit by gas.

Claude Etienne Pasteur, who was Louis Pasteur's paternal grand-

Figure 1-1 – Louis Pasteur's France *(courtesy NMU Cartographic Laboratory)*

father, was a serf. He obtained his freedom in 1763 by paying four pieces of gold. He then became a tanner, as did his son Jean Joseph, the father of Louis.

Joseph was conscripted in 1811 to serve in Spain in Napoleon's Third Regiment. Rising to the rank of sergeant major, he was awarded the Legion of Honor, presented to him by the great soldier himself. A Bonaparte devotee, the former sergeant was downcast when his hero fell.

After his discharge from the army in 1814, Joseph resumed his life as a tanner. He soon married Jeanne Etiennette Roqui. Their surviving children included three daughters and a son. The father's intense patriotism would later manifest itself in that only son who, within half a century, would win the same great honor as Joseph, but for accomplishments of a different sort.

When Louis was very young, the family moved to a rented house in Arbois, where Joseph carried on his trade. The parents instilled in their children high ideals and they themselves provided good role models. Although Joseph's education was limited, he had great respect for learning and entertained ambitions for Louis.

Free education was available in France, and he sent the boy to the Ecole Primaire that was part of the college of Arbois. Later, Louis attended the parent institution. He was a good student, but did not distinguish himself.

Superficial perusal of pages was not for him; he thoroughly digested every word. But apparently such thoroughness was sometimes mistaken for slowness to learn. His case was not unique; the genius of Pasteur's contemporary, Charles Darwin, similarly went unrecognized. However, the headmaster, M. Romanet, recognized Pasteur's superior intellect and began to steer him toward study at the Ecole Normale Supérieure in Paris.

This institution was founded in 1808 by Napoleon and was directed by the Ministry of Public Instruction and Fine Arts. The entrance requirements were exacting, and graduates were committed to ten years of teaching in public institutions. M. Pasteur believed that a professorship would be a great honor for his son.

By the time he was 13, Pasteur was painting portraits. Pastel drawings of his mother and father look to the untrained eye as if they were done by a professional. Yet Pasteur was only 15 when he produced them. Albert Edelfeld, the Finnish artist whose 1887 portrait of Pasteur is well known (Figure 6-1, page 74), studied some of Pasteur's paintings, which were later preserved at the Pasteur Institute. (Pasteur seems to have painted anyone in Arbois who wanted a portrait.) Eldelfeld pronounced Louis' paintings much better than the usual works of young persons ambitious to become artists. He also expressed the opinion that had Pasteur chosen to become involved in art rather than in science, France would have had another competent painter. As it turned out, science claimed so much of Pasteur's energy that drawing became only a secondary, but very useful, talent in advancing his chosen career.

Since Louis had insufficient preparation to enter the Ecole Normale, a family friend arranged for him to attend, at a reduced rate, the preparatory school of a M. Barbet in Paris. The capital city was more than 200 miles from Arbois. Worse still, the Barbet establishment was located in the Latin Quarter. Although the parents had misgivings about their son's living in such a place, they permitted it.

In October, 1838, Louis and a friend left for Paris by stagecoach.

Young Pasteur soon found himself extremely homesick, even yearning for the smell of the tannery. After a few weeks, M. Barbet considered it necessary to communicate his concerns about Louis' well-being to Joseph Pasteur. The father then journeyed to Paris to take his son home.

Once again, young Pasteur set his sights on the great Ecole Normale. In 1839, he entered the College Royal de Besançon, 25 miles away. His father sometimes sold skins in the town, so now there was less reason for homesickness. The youth's immediate goal was to obtain the *baccalauréat.*

In the French system of higher education, this was the first degree, but less advanced than that conferred by an American university. The second degree was *licence,* and this Joseph Pasteur desired for Louis. The highest was *doctorate,* and Louis soon knew that he would settle for no less.

Louis worked hard, obtaining his degree *ès letters* in August, 1840. His examiners noted that he was "very good in elementary science." A few months later, he was hired as a student teacher in mathematics. At the same time, he continued to study for the *baccalauréat ès sciences,* which was required for admission to the scientific section of the Ecole Normale.

At Besançon, Pasteur struck up a friendship with another student named Charles Chappuis, who was also bound for the Ecole Normale. They remained close friends, exchanging confidences and letters throughout their lives.

Since he was the recipient of education denied his sisters who remained at home, Pasteur tried to teach two of them by correspondence. Recognizing his father's desire to learn more, he sent material for Joseph to master and then impart to Josephine, the youngest daughter. A letter from the father noted that he had spent two days working on a problem that later he had considered rather easy; Joseph was finding that teaching what he had just learned was not as trivial as he had supposed.

Louis even offered to pay tuition for Josephine's education by tutoring students at Besançon. His parents did not accept, however, for they wished him to concentrate on his own studies. There may have been another reason, which was explained in a letter to Louis from Joseph. It reported that Josephine had said she had no wish to exert herself mentally. The father promised, however, that by the next holiday, Louis would be pleased with her progress. It is likely that the sisters lacked their brother's love of knowledge and his burning desire to obtain it.

A letter from Pasteur to his sisters advised them in a paternalistic tone that if resolve is firm, a given task will be accomplished. Such expression may seem a bit pompous in a young person, yet toward the end of his life, Pasteur uttered somewhat the same sentiment. From youth, resolution and action were part of his being.

He was examined in August, 1842, before the Dijon Faculty for the *baccalauréat ès sciences.* He passed. And it has long been a consolation for some, as well as a source of mirth, that he was marked *médiocre* in chemistry.

When he took the entrance examinations of the Ecole Normale, he ranked 15th out of 22 candidates. Dissatisfied with a rank so far from the top, he decided on another year of preparatory study.

Charles Chappuis was already in Paris. Pasteur returned to M. Barbet's school, paying only one third of the fee because he instructed some younger students in mathematics. A letter indicated that he was not homesick.

During this time, he was entranced by lectures given at the Sorbonne by Jean-Baptiste André Dumas, the celebrated organic chemist. Dumas' enthusiasm for his subject aroused in Pasteur the desire to be a chemist himself, and throughout his life he remained a great admirer of Dumas.

In response to parental worry about the temptations of the Latin Quarter, Pasteur assured his mother and father that strength of will was the important issue; when a man desires to walk the straight and narrow it can be done as well in the Latin Quarter as in any other place.

He took long walks with Chappuis. They often dined together and sometimes they attended the theater or the opera. Although Chappuis' chosen field was philosophy, the two young men were apparently in tune intellectually.

In 1843, Pasteur was admitted to the Ecole Normale Supérieure with a high rank; the extra year had paid off. He was so anxious to begin, that he arrived from Arbois a few days before the start of classes. At 21, he was a serious, hard working student who *enjoyed* learning. He soon discovered the library and began to use it to his advantage.

Figure 1-2 – Louis Pasteur as a student at the Ecole Normale.
(Courtesy Pasteur Institute)

Joseph Pasteur took immense interest in his son's progress, and Louis, in turn, wrote his family detailed letters about his life at the fine institution. When he decided he could spare a little time to help some of M. Barbet's students, his father was delighted. In a letter to Louis, the elder Pasteur noted that this was a way to express gratitude to M. Barbet and encouraged his aiding other young students whose future might depend on help from Barbet.

By the fall of 1846, Pasteur had passed the *licence* examination, earning the pronouncement, "He will make an excellent professor." His research for the *doctorate* centered on the structure of crystals, which would provide a foundation for the first of many brilliant investigations. He formally completed the doctoral requirements in 1847.

M. Romanet requested that Pasteur give some lectures at the college of Arbois during vacation. He was to speak of great French scientists, among whom Pasteur, as one of Besançon's star pupils, would one day be counted. That head master was indeed perceptive. Incidentally, Pasteur showed much interest in the lives of notable men such as great scientists and patriots.

Chappuis already realized that his friend would go far. So did Antoine Jérôme Balard, lecturer at the Ecole and the man who had discovered the element bromine. He took on Pasteur as his laboratory assistant and would play a role in the younger man's professional future.

The year 1848 saw a citizen revolt that deposed Louis Philippe, who had come to power in 1830. Pasteur enthusiastically supported the new regime, emphasizing that he was prepared to fight courageously for the sacred cause of the Republic. He became a member of a military organization and, though he had little money, also contributed to the cause. In December, Napoleon Bonaparte's nephew, Louis Napoleon Bonaparte, was elected President of the Second Republic.

The same year brought great sorrow to Pasteur: his mother died suddenly. Little is known about Jeanne Roqui Pasteur, although many years after her death, her then famous son declared that her enthusiasm had been passed on to him. As we shall see, enthusiasm was a characteristic that would distinguish Pasteur, and at the same time, prove a valuable asset.

In the course of his study of crystals, Pasteur became interested in what is now known as their optical activity.

To begin a discussion of crystallography, it is important to know that the evaporation of a liquid in which a substance is dissolved will produce crystals with a strikingly characteristic microscopic appearance. Table salt, for example, crystallizes in distinct cubes. Some crystals can affect polarized light, which is a beam in which the vibrations of the electromagnetic waves are confined to one plane by passage through the prism system of an instrument known as the polarimeter. Depending on the molecular configuration of the crystal under examination, its solution may twist polarized light to the left or to the right to a measurable degree. A substance that does this is optically active; if there is no twisting, the crystal is optically inactive.

Pasteur's work on optical activity revolved around tartaric acid (figure 1-3). This acid was discovered in 1769 in deposits found in wine casks. Another form of tartaric acid was found later and named racemic acid (sometimes called paratartaric acid).

Eilhardt Mitscherlich, a German chemist of note, had declared that the two forms were identical *except that solutions of tartrates were optically active, a property not shown by solutions of racemates.* His results were confirmed by Jean-Baptist Biot of the Collège de France, who was an authority on the rotatory properties of solutions. Mitscherlich's findings were read, with his permission, by Biot to the French Academy of Science in 1844.

Pasteur came upon the information in the Ecole's library. Realizing that there was inconsistency here, he resolved to investigate the problem when he had time.

Two years later, when he was at work in Balard's laboratory, a scientist named Auguste Laurent showed him some crystalline sodium tungstate that was a mixture of three varieties of microscopic crystals. Pasteur did not forget this.

Eventually, he found time to prepare and crystallize 19 salts of tartaric and racemic acid. He observed that the minute, racemic crystals were consistently a mixture of two kinds, with facets so oriented that each was a mirror image of the other; they were not identical because they were not superimposable. Pasteur said they showed dissymmetry, the modern term for which is *chirality.*

Pasteur separated the two types by hand. He found that in the polarimeter, solutions of one type of the crystals rotated to the right while solutions of the other type of crystals rotated to the left. Clearly those that caused right rotation were identical to those of tartaric acid, which was dextrorotatory. Then he showed that racemic acid, which is a combination of the two active forms of tartaric acid, was optically inactive because when equal weights of the two types were mixed, one neutralized the rotatory power of the other.

When the 25-year-old Pasteur solved the problem that had confounded two older, established, and distinguished scientists, he rushed from the laboratory into the hall.

There he embraced a passerby, telling him excitedly that he had just made a great discovery. He was shaking all over from happiness and couldn't even read the scale on the polarimeter.

It *was* a great discovery. From our viewpoint, it is difficult to envision the conditions under which Pasteur had worked. Nine-

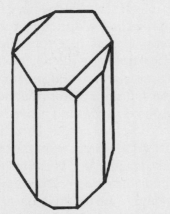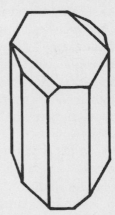

Figure 1-3 – Diagram of sodium ammonium tartrate crystals published in 1850 by Louis Pasteur. Note the right- and left-handedness. (From Applequist, 1987)

teenth-century laboratories bore no resemblance to laboratories of today. Pasteur had to construct whatever equipment he needed; he had no assistant, and such tasks were very time consuming. A greater barrier was the lack of knowledge of molecular structure. The British astronomer, Sir John Herschel, had suggested that right-handed and left-handed facets in quartz crystals could be responsible for right and left rotations, but he had failed to submit proof. In science, credit generally goes to the man or woman who convinces the world, and without experimental proof, Pasteur's world remained unconvinced.

When Biot learned the news via Balard, he wanted a demonstration, using his own solution of racemic acid. Pasteur complied, showing the old man the mirror-image crystals that produced rotations in opposite directions.

Biot, then 74, was not jealous. He explained to the younger man that a great love of science made the discovery dear to his heart.

After Pasteur had communicated his results to the Academy of Sciences, Biot, along with Balard and scientist Henri Victor Regnault, reported their complete approval. Until the end of his life, Biot remained Pasteur's mentor.

The importance of Pasteur's research on crystals cannot be overemphasized. Today, the spacial relationships of molecules are fundamental to our understanding of chemical and biochemical reactions, thus making Pasteur one of the pioneers of the science of stereochemistry.

Of greater significance was the fact that this work gave Pasteur confidence in his manner of approaching a difficult problem – an approach he would apply not only to inanimate substances, but to living cells, as well. He became familiar with what was already known; he made excellent deductions about the information at hand; and, blessed with keen observation and superb intuition, he designed and executed reproducible experiments that would prove or disprove his hypotheses.

In addition to his intellectual gifts, Pasteur would exhibit emotional qualities that were to his advantage. He was enthusiastic about whatever he was working on, and unsatisfactory or disappointing results did not seriously daunt him. He had patience. He also possessed a fighting spirit and the capacity to work untiringly.

Keep in mind that Pasteur had been educated by the French government to teach. Balard had once intervened when Pasteur, with a *licence*, was to be sent to teach physics at the Tournon Lycée, located almost 300 miles away from the Ecole Normale.

But now Pasteur had the *doctorate* and there was a vacancy to be filled. The Minister of Public Instruction made him a Professor of Physics at the Dijon Lycée. However, the young scientist was allowed to remain in Paris until November, 1848, to finish some studies with Biot.

The *lycée* is a secondary school, not a university. Pasteur was required to teach first and second year students. There were 80 first year students and Pasteur reported a concern echoed by contemporary teachers: toward the end of the lesson, he was having difficulty keeping the attention of his students. Clearly the position was not to his liking, although he was making an effort to do a good job.

Back in Paris, Biot and Balard were exerting pressure to have their young colleague better placed. Unexpectedly, there was an opening at the Université de Strasbourg. Pasteur arrived there on January 15, 1849, to assume his duties as Professor of Chemistry.

Chapter 2

SOLVING PROBLEMS

Pasteur immediately paid a call on the university's head, M. Laurent. At the Laurent home, he met Mlle. Marie, one of the daughters. On February 10, 1849, Pasteur wrote her father for permission to marry her. The letter stated that he could offer only good health, some courage, and his university position; he expected to devote himself entirely to chemical research and hoped in 10 or 15 years to be able to return to Paris. In the laboratory, patience was one of Pasteur's assets; he showed none of this now.

Joseph Pasteur journeyed to Strasbourg to make a formal proposal on behalf of his son. He brought with him Josephine, who remained in Strasbourg to keep house for her brother until he married. Her stay on earth would be short though; she died in 1850.

The wedding took place on May 29, 1849. Marie Laurent was then 22, four years younger than Louis. Throughout their lives together she devoted herself to his career, protecting him as much as she could from family misfortunes and worries. She interested herself in his investigations and frequently took down his dictation about scientific matters. She appears to have submerged her own identity in his. Their first child, Jeanne, was born in 1850.

The country Jeanne was born into at mid-century had a population around 33 million; old-age insurance was being instituted; the French physicist Armand Fizeau had devised the first terrestrial method to measure the speed of light; Jean Francois Millet had finished *The Sower*. In Prussia, a liberal constitution was adopted. In

Figure 2-2 – Louis Pasteur as a professor at Strasbourg.
(Courtesy National Library of Medicine)

England, Dickens' *David Copperfield* and Elizabeth Barrett Browning's *Sonnets from the Portugese* were being read. In the United States, Millard Fillimore succeeded to the presidency when cholera felled Zachary Taylor. Amelia Bloomer was trying to reform women's dress and Nathaniel Hawthorne's masterpiece, *The Scarlet Letter*, was published. The population of the United States had reached the 23-million mark, and, as California entered the union as a free state, the slavery issue loomed menacingly in the background.

Pasteur continued his active study of chirality until 1858. After that, the subject was always in the back of his mind. When one of his racemic acid solutions became contaminated with a mold, he found that the right-rotating form was destroyed. This observation provided a method for producing one of the two forms.

Alexander Fleming, some 70 years later, made a significant discovery from a similar turn of events. He noticed the mold that produces penicillin when it contaminated one of his bacterial cultures. Most laboratory workers would discard anything contaminated with mold. But not Pasteur or Fleming. Fleming made further investigations that convinced him of penicillin's possibilities, although he apparently did not grasp the full significance of his discovery. He was unable to purify the substance, but he published his findings. He also kept the mold growing until others made the necessary purification. Expressing an idea borrowed from Pasteur, Fleming, when he was famous, warned that the unprepared mind cannot see the outstretched hand of opportunity.

Pasteur assumed that the living mold possessed a peculiar dissymmetry. Always in the back of his mind was the idea "that the structure of substances, in terms of their molecular symmetry or dissymmetry, must have much to do with the innermost laws of the structure of living creatures." This idea that asymmetric molecules are produced by living cells would lead him to biological investigations.

In 1853, Pasteur won a prize offered two years previously by the

Figure 2-1 – Alexander Fleming, 1881-1955
(Courtesy National Library of Medicine)

13

Paris Pharmaceutical Society for his work on tartaric acid. He used one half of the 1500-franc purse to buy needed equipment for his laboratory.

The same year saw France embroiled in the Crimean War, which would last until 1856. Louis Napoleon Bonaparte had proclaimed himself emperor – Napoleon III. An autocrat at home, his policies abroad were confused.

Although Pasteur revolutionized science, his political views tended to be conservative. According to his own statement, he had, and intended always to have, no political bias. His only desire was to be a citizen, a worker devoted to his country.

The Strasbourg period saw Pasteur gain fame in France and other European countries – he had travelled to Germany, Austria, and Italy in search of samples of tartaric acid and to observe their sites of formation. His publications and letters to scientists kept them aware of his progress. Early in 1853, one entire meeting of the Academy of Sciences dealt with Pasteur and his work.

At the Pasteur home there were two more additions: Jean Baptiste, born in 1851 and Cécile the following year.

In September, 1854, the Minister of Public Instruction showed his great confidence in Pasteur by appointing him Professor and Dean of the new School of Sciences at Lille. This city was a center of industry in the north of France.

An imperial decree had brought about two innovations at the new school. For a small fee, a student could now personally carry out certain laboratory experiments that the instructor had demonstrated to a class. The other innovation was the granting of a two-year diploma to students entering industrial careers.

Pasteur was enthusiastic about his new position. He supported practical science but was firm about the importance of theory. "Without theory, practice is but routine born of habit," he said in his opening speech. He used the telegraph as an example of theory put into practice. A physicist at the University of Copenhagen named Hans Christian Oersted had been in the habit of demonstrating that there was no connection between electricity and magnetism. He did this by placing a current-carrying wire at right angles to and directly over a magnetized needle. One day he fortuitously placed the wire parallel to the compass.

... he suddenly saw (by chance, you will say, but chance only favors the mind which is prepared) the needle move and take up a position quite different from the one assigned to it by terrestrial magnetism. A wire carrying an electrical current deviates a magnetized needle from its position. That, gentlemen, was the birth of the modern telegraph . . . . And [Oersted's] discovery was barely twenty years old when it produced by its application the almost supernatural effects of the electric telegraph!

Pasteur exemplified the dictum that chance favors the prepared mind.

A letter written a year later to Chappuis provides insights into Pasteur's activities at Lille. From 200 to 300 people attended his most popular lectures and twenty-one students were enrolled for laboratory experiments. On the ground floor he had what he always wanted – a laboratory available to him at all times. He had taken on, at the suggestion of the Conseil-General, the testing of manures for the northern area of France. This area included much agricultural land, so the task was considerable, but Pasteur believed that in accepting it, he would enhance his institution's reputation.

He also provided opportunities for students to visit factories, foundries, and steel works with him in nearby French towns and in Belgium.

From the start, the Minister of Public Instruction was pleased with Pasteur's efforts. Writing to the rector of the university, he stated that Lille's School of Sciences now rivaled the best of other institutions and owed it "to the merit of the teaching – solid and brilliant at the same time – of that clever Professor." He then added a cautionary note: "M. Pasteur must be sure that his love of science does not run him astray." Although teaching at the School of Science was of necessity to be based on up-to-date scientific theory, its primary aim was to produce practical applications in line with the needs of the area.

The distilleries in the area had a problem. One of the owners, M. Bigo, told Pasteur that when he and others fermented beet juice with yeast, the process sometimes went awry, with little alcohol being formed. Pasteur agreed to investigate.

Today we know that yeast cells contain protein catalysts called enzymes that act on beet sugar to produce ultimately ethyl alcohol and carbon dioxide as the main products. Yeast cells are microscopic organisms belonging to the plant kingdom. They were first observed in 1680 by the Dutch naturalist, Anton van Leeuwenhoek, with his famous microscope. By 1835, Cagniard de La Tour, the French physicist who invented the siren, had shown that yeast consists of small rounded bodies that grow and multiply by budding and fission (figure 3-1). He believed that yeast growth brought about fermentation of sugar. Theodor Schwann, the great German biologist, had independently made experiments that led him to the same conclusion. These two were correct in their assumptions. But the leading chemists of the 1850s were not inclined to believe that living organisms played a crucial role in alcohol fermentation. It was now up to Pasteur to determine the facts and propose a solution.

Pasteur made frequent visits to the factories, returning to his laboratory with samples for examination and experiment. A letter from Mme. Pasteur to Joseph Pasteur, her father-in-law, stated, "Louis . . . is now up to his neck in beet juice." Pasteur also cut his lectures to one a week to give himself more time to devote to the problem, which took him frequently to the distilleries.

Pasteur found that M. Bigo's beet juice had been invaded with an organism that produced lactic acid, an acid that forms in sour milk, as its end product. Lactic acid had been discovered in 1780. (We know now that some bacteria and molds produce lactic acid from the sugar glucose.) According to Bigo's son, "Pasteur had noticed through the microscope that the globules were round when fermentation was healthy, that they were lengthened when alteration began, and were quite long when fermentation became lactic. This very simple method allowed us to watch the process and to avoid the failures in fermentation we used so often to meet with . . . ."

Practical methods for obtaining pure cultures were in the future, but Pasteur had found extraneous organisms as the cause of the trouble. Now it could be foretold if lactic, rather than alcoholic, fermentation were going to take place.

In August, 1857, Pasteur presented his findings to the Lille Scientific Society. His results were extremely important because he expressed the belief *that specific microorganisms bring about specific chemical reactions.* He would extend his work on alcoholic fermentation, but already his ideas were leading him to investigate the role of microorganisms in disease.

During 1857, Pasteur had lost an election to the French Academy of Sciences, but had been awarded the Rumford Medal of the Royal Society of London for his crystallography studies. In November, he was appointed administrator and director of scientific studies at his *alma mater,* the Ecole Normale Supérieure.

There Pasteur continued his fermentation studies, finding that besides lactic acid, sometimes butyric acid was the chief end product, rather than alcohol. Butyric acid appears in rancid butter and is most easily recognized by its abominable smell. With the aid of the microscope, he determined that the organism involved was a motile bacterium, not a yeast (We must realize that there was no classification of microorganisms, so that, at that time, Pasteur had little knowledge of their morphology; also that differential staining, so helpful in identification, was yet to come.) To examine the fermenting liquid in question, he placed a drop on a glass slide, shielding it with a cover slip. He noted, to his surprise, that the organisms at the edges of the preparation became immobile in contrast to those at the center, which retained their mobility.

Although it was foreign to the thinking of the day, Pasteur reasoned that oxygen must be harmful to the butyric organism, and he pursued the idea. When he passed a current of air through a flask containing the organisms, butyric acid fermentation stopped, backing up his hypothesis. With the aid of the Ecole's professor of Greek, he coined the adjective *anaerobic* to describe fermentation in the absence of oxygen, and *aerobic* to describe fermentation in its presence.

Pasteur was able to show conclusively that alcoholic fermentation was due to the growth and activity of specific microorganisms, a conclusion that would greatly influence his future thinking. He showed that the utilization of carbohydrate is much greater under anaerobic conditions − a fact known in biochemistry as the Pasteur effect.

Conditions at the Ecole Normale were not conducive to research. Since Balard's old laboratory, the only one in the building, was occupied, the new director of scientific studies had to improvise. He was handicapped by the fact that he had no equipment and no assistant. He found two attic rooms and paid for the necessary equipment himself. In summer, the new laboratory was unbearably hot. He wrote Chappuis that he would be working on fermentation if a temperature of 36°C (almost 97° Fahrenheit) did not keep him out of his laboratory. He regretted that he was not able to take advantage of the time of year with so much light.

In time, he was granted assistants and better quarters. However, the fact that he was able to overcome the physical deficiencies of his environment is a tribute to his perseverance.

Keen as Pasteur was about his research, he did not forget his administrative duties. Notes have been found that show his attention was directed toward classroom ventilation, the amount of meat required per pupil, repair of the dining hall door, and so on.

Another daughter, Marie Louise, was born to the Pasteurs in 1858. The next year, their eldest child, Jeanne, died. Late in December, 1859, Pasteur wrote his father that the end of the year brought thoughts of the beloved child, adding that she was now beyond troubles. He resolved to think of those who were left and to do his best to protect them from the bitterness of life.

The Academy of Sciences awarded Pasteur its 1859 Prize for Experimental Physiology. The eminent physiologist, Claude Bernard, presented the report, remarking on "that physiological tendency in Pasteur's researches."

By now, Pasteur had involved himself in the controversy over spontaneous generation. Today we accept the idea of biogenesis — that life, as we encounter it at the present stage of evolution, comes from preexisting life. Since ancient times, however, various people had held to the belief that life arose from nonliving matter, calling such *de novo* creation of life, spontaneous. As far back as 1668, Francesco Redi had shown that maggots appearing in decaying meat were not, as widely believed, created from the meat; if flies were prohibited from laying their eggs on the meat, there were no maggots, thus indicating that the maggots had not arisen spontaneously from the putrifying meat. Various other experiments seemed to spell doom for the theory of spontaneous generation.

However, in 1745, John Tuberville Needham, a priest, published *An Account of Some New Microscopical Discoveries,* in which he claimed that microscopic forms arose in a liquid even after intense heating for 30 minutes. In 1775, another biologist priest, Lazzaro Spallanzini, refuted this, contending that Needham's sealing was faulty (Needham had used cork stoppers) and that he had not heated the liquid properly. When Spallanzini made his vessels airtight and kept them in boiling water for 60 minutes, there was no growth in the contained liquid.

Some were still unconvinced, among them Felix Archimede Pouchet, Director of the Museum of Natural History at Rouen. In a letter to the Academy of Sciences, Professor Pouchet wrote that he was prepared to demonstrate that "animals and plants could be generated in a medium absolutely free of atmospheric air, and in which, therefore, no germ of organic bodies could have been brought by air."

Pouchet's method was to take a flask containing boiling water, make it airtight and then plunge it upside down into a mercury bath. When the water cooled, he opened the flask under mercury, introducing pure oxygen or oxygen and nitrogen (simulated air) and a hay infusion which was supposedly sterile. Invariably there was growth in a few days; the previously clear solution became cloudy and microscopic examination revealed the presence of microorganisms.

Pasteur's fermentation studies cast some doubt on the theory of spontaneous generation; the specificity of reactions exhibited by microorganisms suggested inheritance rather than random appearance, as would take place with spontaneous generation. But he had an open mind on the subject. Pouchet's challenge proved too tempting for Pasteur to resist, and against the advice of Biot and Dumas, he began an investigation that would last four years.

People with strong religious convictions tended to line up behind the biogenesis theory, and Pasteur has been accused of refuting Pouchet for this reason. René Dubos, the distinguished investigator and one of Pasteur's biographers, considers this unfair. According to Hilaire Cuny, author of the 1963 book, *Louis Pasteur; The Man and His Theories*, there was small justification for considering Pasteur a Catholic scientist. Pasteur himself said that religion, philosophy, atheism, materialism, or spiritualism did not matter to him as a scientist; he considered facts. For this reason, he was, in the beginning, ready to accept spontaneous generation provided that he could be convinced by experiments. After he had investigated the problem to his satisfaction, he looked on those who had supported spontaneous generation as if they were blindfolded. Also, Pasteur was always intrigued with the question of the origin of life, and he was unlikely to accept religious dogma that did not fit facts which were meaningful to a scientist.

By now, Pasteur had a better laboratory and what we would call a graduate student to assist him in his research. With the aid of an aspirator, he concentrated the particulate matter in air on a filter and studied it under the microscope. It was clear that the number of bodies in the sediment depended on where the aspirator had been placed during the sampling. The dust recovered always produced growth when added to a suitable sterile (denoting the complete absence of microorganisms) culture medium.

Pasteur conducted numerous experiments pertaining to spontaneous generation. In contrast to Pouchet's hay infusion, he used a yeast infusion. Scientists had been interested in his use of the so-called swan-necked flask (figure 2-3). After the infusion was poured into a flask, its long neck was heated and drawn into an *S*. On boiling the contents, air was forced out through the neck opening. When it mixed with moisture condensed in the neck curve, particulate matter was trapped. As the infusion cooled, the "cleaned" air returned to the flask. There was no growth in the infusion over a period of time. But if the neck of the flask were broken, causing an in rush of air, growth

Figure 2-3 — Pasteur's swan-neck flasks. *(Courtesy Pasteur Institute)*

would take place in the infusion. Combining the trapped material with the larger volume in the flask also produced growth. Balard is credited with the idea of this ingenious experiment.

During a vacation in 1860, Pasteur took flasks to the Alps. He had considered using a balloon ascent to show that the higher the altitude, the less contaminated is the air. Deciding on the mountains instead, he hired a guide with a mule to move a case of his flasks from Chamonix up Mont Blanc. He walked beside the mule, steadying the case with his hand. Although he ran into unforeseen difficulties which he managed to overcome, he obtained valuable data: out of 20 flasks opened on the glacier known as the Mer de Glace (6,600 feet) only one showed growth. This was in contrast to his findings on Mont Poupet, at an altitude of 2,800 feet, where five of 20 flasks contained organisms.

That same year, the Academy of Sciences offered a prize for contributions that would "attempt, by means of well-defined experiments, to throw new light on the question of spontaneous generation." Some considered that the question involved the origin of life, and Frenchmen from various walks of life followed the reports with interest and emotion.

In 1863, Pouchet and his cohorts announced that they could not duplicate Pasteur's findings. They had been to the Pyrenees instead of the Alps, and found that "whenever a liter of air was collected and brought into contact with an organic liquid, in a flask hermetically sealed, the fluid soon revealed the development of living organisms."

In an attempt to resolve the discrepancies, the Academy appointed a commission to investigate both Pasteur's and Pouchet's experiments. Pouchet's group would not agree to the terms and finally withdrew.

Pasteur and his assistants, on the other hand, came to a laboratory in the Museum of Natural History to demonstrate their findings with flair. Pasteur showed three of the flasks he had opened in the mountains three years before – all still sterile. One was opened and its gas analyzed, yielding 21% oxygen, the amount found in air. When the second was opened, growth was present after three days. The third was kept on exhibit. Sixty more flasks were prepared in the presence of the commission and used to demonstrate that air from a variety of locales contained microorganisms.

This ended the controversy for the time being. But there was irony here. Since nothing was known about the existence of heat-resistant spores, Pouchet had depended on the assumption-of-the-day that a temperature of 100°C (the boiling point of water) would kill all microorganisms. It just happened that his hay infusion was extremely difficult to sterilize, and his procedure was inadequate. Since Pasteur's yeast infusion was very sensitive to heat, his procedure was adequate for the case at hand. However, had his method been applied to the hay infusion, he would have obtained Pouchet's results.

In 1862, Pasteur was awarded the Academy of Sciences prize for his studies on spontaneous generation; he was also elected a member of that body. A year earlier, he had had enough confidence to tell the academy, "If all the results so far obtained by me are considered together, they enable us, in my opinion, to state definitely that the dusts suspended in the atmosphere are the exclusive origin, the initial, indispensable condition, for the existence of life in the infusions."

More important, there was a hint of destiny in the same talk; he suggested that it would be most desirable to extend these studies as a preparation for serious research into the origin of different diseases.

In April, 1864, when he was 41, Pasteur lectured at the Sorbonne on spontaneous generation. The large crowd present included personages such as George Sand and Alexander Dumas. Pasteur's opening sentences are interesting today because they reflect the influence of Darwin and Wallace, among others:

> Great problems are now being handled, keeping every thinking man in suspense; the unity or multiplicity of human races; the creation of man 1,000 years or 1,000 centuries ago, the fixity of species, or the slow and progressive transformation of one species into another; the eternity of matter; the idea of a God as unnecessary.

Orleans was a center for the production of French vinegar. Partially filled casks containing wine and partly processed vinegar were left to ferment. (The word vinegar comes from the French *vin*, meaning wine, and *aigre*, meaning sour.) A thin film normally developed on the surface, and the manufacturers knew from experience that it required air. When this film sank or became otherwise displaced, the fermentation process stopped prematurely. Often, mishaps such as this occurred, causing severe economic loss over a period of time. Obviously, next to nothing was known about the theoretical basis of this fermentation process.

In 1862, Pasteur decided to investigate, proceeding in his usual style. In less than a year, he had obtained valuable results. With his microscope, he determined that the film consisted of minute organisms. He found that, in five days, one gram of the organisms could convert 10,000 times their weight into acetic acid, the acid that characterizes vinegar. (The ethyl alcohol in the wine was oxidized to acetic acid.) Sometimes the process stopped before acetic acid was produced, leaving products with a disagreeable smell. Sometimes the reaction went beyond the acetic acid stage, breaking it down to water and carbonic acid. With such knowledge, the manufacturers could control the process better, saving themselves millions of francs.

This work illustrated one of Pasteur's fundamental beliefs: "There does not exist a category of sciences to which we give the name of 'applied sciences.' There are science and the applications of science, the latter related to the former as the fruit to the tree which bore it."

Each year, France produced about one-and-a-third billion gallons of wine. However, these wines were subject to a number of diseases that adversely affected the flavor and often made them unfit to drink. The economic loss became so great that Napoleon III requested Pasteur's help.

During the summer vacation in 1864, Pasteur went to Arbois to study the problem. He took with him one of his assistants, Emile Duclaux, who was destined to direct the great institute that would later be founded to honor his chief. In an improvised laboratory, Pasteur made his usual systematic approach. First, with the microscope, he examined samples of wine with different diseases. In each case, he found a different extraneous organism.

In the beginning, he tried to treat the contaminated wines with bisulfites and other compounds intended to arrest bacterial growth. He soon abandoned this in favor of partial sterilization by rapid heating to about 130° Fahrenheit with air excluded.

This latter process is, of course, the basis of what is familiar to us as pasteurization. It is now used to preserve beer, cider, vinegar, milk, and countless other products. The knowledge that heat retarded spoilage predated Pasteur's work and was applied empirically. When Pasteur tried it, his aim was to kill unwanted organisms without affecting the taste of the wine. Through experimentation, he succeeded in finding an effective temperature. But he did not stop there. His treatises on the subject provided drawings and photographs of low-cost equipment adapted for the large volumes used in industry.

He also had an official commission of wine tasters sample heated and unheated wines of different types over a period of years and publish their reports. Even the French Navy took part in his experiments: a ship leaving Brest had aboard about 250 quarts of heated wine and 250 quarts of the same wine unheated. When the vessel returned 10 months later, the unheated wine was astringent and acid, while the heated wine had an excellent flavor.

The heat method was quickly accepted in France and beyond, and its originator was awarded the Grand Prize of the International Exposition of 1867. Pasteur was delighted to learn that a wine maker in California was subjecting 100,000 liters of his wine to the new French process – this in a land where 20 years previously the grapevine was nonexistent.

When there was criticism that he had done nothing new, Pasteur was quick to make public reply to his detractors. For example, he was told that, in Mèze, heating wine was a common practice. When he went there to investigate, he found that the wine makers did heat, but their purpose was to age the wine more rapidly and not related to microbial growth.

> These gropings about in the dark show that the wine merchants of Mèze do not have any clear idea of what they are about, and have not read my book [*Etudes sur le vin*]," he declared. "It would be to their interest to do so, for I give the theory of their practice. Moreover, what does this long and dangerous warming in contact with air have in common with the rapid heating to 50°C [122°F] protected from the air, that I recommend?

Pasteur was prone to deal harshly with his critics.

In his personal life, there was a birth and two deaths. A

daughter, Camille, was born in 1863 and died two years later. Joseph Pasteur died in 1865. A letter from Pasteur to his wife expressed his deep love and understanding of his father, also his sense of obligation to the man who had sacrificed much to see his son educated.

Later, Pasteur said in a public tribute:

> And you, my dear father, whose life was as hard as your hard trade, you have shown what patience in long labors can accomplish. It is to you that I owe persistence in daily tasks. Not only did you have the qualities of perseverance which make useful lives, but you have also the admiration for great men and great things. To look upward, to learn more and more, to seek always to rise, – these are the things which you taught me.

Another tragedy befell the Pasteur family; Cécile, Pasteur's daughter of fourteen years, died in 1866.

At this time, France's silk industry was close to ruin because of a long-lasting epidemic. Dumas was serving as a Senator from a badly hit region in the south of France when he enlisted the aid of his famous protege.

Pasteur agreed to investigate the matter despite the fact that he knew nothing about entomology. He first went to Alais (now Alès) in the summer of 1865, returning to Paris when the silkworm season was over. The next winter he returned with three assistants and was later joined by his family.

The silk worm is the larva of a large moth. When it becomes a pupa, it spins itself a cocoon of silk. Silk worm disease had become threatening as early as 1842. France was not the only country invaded by the disease; silkworm disease had appeared in Italy, Spain, Austria, and China. By 1864, healthy eggs were available only from Japan. All stages of development were affected. No treatment had been successful, and there was no scientific knowledge about the cause of the disease. For some time, the problem proved baffling and discouraging to Pasteur, too.

For two years, he contended erroneously that pébrine was a physiological hereditary disease. Pébrine got its name from the black spots that resembled grains of black pepper in the infected worm's

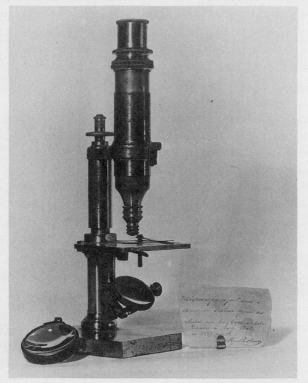

Figure 2-4 – The microscope Pasteur used to study silkworm disease.
(Courtesy Pasteur Institute)

skin. Various observers had reported these small oval bodies (corpuscles) occurring when there was disease at any stage of the life cycle. On the other hand, sometimes the worms became sick, presumably with pébrine, but without the appearance of such corpuscles.

Pasteur's previous experience had been with yeasts and bacteria. These corpuscles were neither, leading him to the belief that they were not the cause of pébrine, but rather pathological degenerations due to the disease. Curiously, his assistants had deduced correctly that the corpuscles were infectious, and these men were amazed that Pasteur had not made the connection. We know now that pébrine is caused by a nonbacterial parasite called *Nosema bombycis.*

Pasteur did advocate selecting out eggs free of corpuscles as a means of eliminating the disease. Sometimes this was successful, but often it was not. It is clear that, as complaints and criticisms rolled in, he felt a sense of desperation.

Then he made a significant discovery: there was a second disease that was killing the worms. He never found the cause of this malady, know as flacherie, characterized by flaccid worms, but he determined that by disposing of these sickly worms, it could be stamped out. According to Dubos, the causative bacterium of true flacherie was *Bacillus bombycis.*

Corpuscle-free eggs did produce good silk, provided there was no infection with flacherie. Pasteur had been misled at first because often the two diseases had appeared in the same worm. The entire investigation lasted for five years. During this time Pasteur learned to breed silkworms himself and was in time able to supply eggs free of both diseases to those who needed them. He also introduced improved environmental conditions that cut down the incidence of flacherie. In 1870, he published a book on silkworm diseases. His recommendations – especially the microscopic examination of eggs – were not readily accepted by silkworm growers. Although he constantly fought ignorance and criticism, he won out, and prosperity returned to sericulture.

In 1868, when he was 46, Pasteur suffered a cerebral hemorrhage which permanently paralyzed his left arm and leg. He was incapacitated for three months, but then returned to Alais to continue work on the perplexing silkworm problem.

Chapter 3

THE WORLD OF THE INFINITELY SMALL

Although the cerebral hemorrhage left some permanent paralysis, Pasteur's mental activity was unimpaired; in fact, his greatest work was yet to come. It did mean a greater dependence on assistants to carry out technical tasks, for he could no longer use his left hand.

In 1867, he had been appointed professor of chemistry at the Sorbonne. Having convinced Napoleon III of the importance of research, he had at last a suitable laboratory at the Ecole Normale. Now he was relieved of his administrative duties and able to devote more time to scientific investigation.

The Franco-Prussian War in 1871-72 caused Pasteur great torment. He was worried because his son, 18-year-old Jean-Baptiste Pasteur, was involved in the fighting. The war prevented the senior Pasteur from working in the new laboratory and forced his return to Arbois. On reading of the Prussian bombardment of the left bank of the Seine, feelings of hatred and revenge replaced his admiration for Germany, and he returned to the University of Bonn the honorary degree of Doctor of Medicine that he had so proudly accepted in 1863. He felt anguish for his beloved country as it went down in defeat.

The war deposed Napoleon III and brought about the establishment of the Third French Republic. At the same time, the German Empire came into being, and the seeds of World War I were planted.

In the postwar years, Pasteur continued his studies on fermentation. He was also occupied with improving French beer, publishing his *Etudes sur la bière (Studies on beer)* in 1876. The next year, he began investigations that would have enormous influence on the control of human infectious disease.

By 1877, great progress was being made in other fields of science. For instance, Alexander Graham Bell had just invented the telephone. The United States had survived a terrible civil war and celebrated the first hundred years of its existence as an independent nation; the Brooklyn Bridge was opened; and Thomas Edison's phonograph was about to delight all who had the opportunity to hear it.

In a banner performance in 1878, Pasteur addressed the Academy of Medicine on the germ theory of infection, and his paper included Jules Joubert and Charles Chamberland as coauthors. He referred to diseases as "transmissible, contagious infections, of which the cause resides essentially and solely in the presence of microscopic organisms." He warned against the acceptance of the hypothesis of spontaneous generation and "many other conceptions not founded on observation."

Pasteur needed no motivation for his new research. Tuberculosis, diphtheria, whooping cough, typhoid fever, cerebrospinal meningitis, and other diseases little known today in the developed world were common in Europe and the United States. Women died of infection after childbirth; bone fractures became infected, often causing deaths; and great epidemics occurred with frequency, taking the lives of thousands. Statistics from the Crimean War for the years 1854-56 illustrate the state of affairs: in the French Army of 300,000, 3 percent were killed due to the effects of war, while 28 percent died from disease. This grouping included cholera, typhus, typhoid, and wound infections.

Physicians could do little or nothing to prevent or treat such disasters because the causes were not understood. The germ theory of disease was yet to come; facts about microorganisms familiar to today's seventh grade students were unknown to the leading medical men of the day. People accepted their misfortunes as the will of God.

Such a situation was, of course, a challenge to a man of Pasteur's intellect. From a personal perspective, he had experienced firsthand

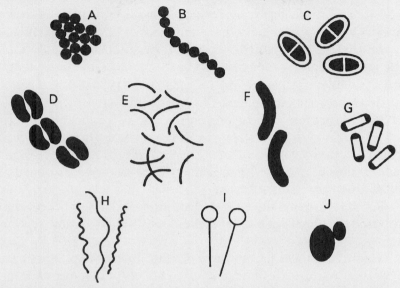

Figure 3-1 — Diagramatic representations of microorganisms as they appear under the light microscope. A. *Staphylococcus aureus.* B. *Streptococcus pyrogenes.* C. *Streptococcus pneumoniae.* D. *Neisseria meningitidus.* E. *Corynebacterium diphtherae.* F. *Vibrio cholerae.* G. *Yersinia pestis.* H. Spirochetes. I. *Clostridium tetani.* J. Budding yeast cells.

the tragedy involved: three of his daughters had died during their childhood, two of them from typhoid. At a young age, his oldest sister had become severely retarded following an illness. The nature of that illness is not known, but it is likely that some infectious disease was at fault.

Microorganisms — to use the term that Pasteur preferred — cannot ordinarily be seen with the naked eye.* Most bacteria, for example, are about 3 micrometers in diameter. Microorganisms of medical importance include bacteria, fungi, viruses, and protozoa.

Microorganisms are everywhere — in soil, in water, on the skin, and so on. Some are harmless; some are necessary and beneficial. Bacteria are important to agriculture; without them the nitrogen of the air would not be converted to a form needed by plants. Intestinal bacteria make vitamin K, a substance involved in the clotting of

---

*In 1993, there was a report of a large, morphologically peculiar organism named *Epulopiscium fishelsoni* that inhabits the intestinal tract of a surgeonfish species from the Red Sea and the Great Barrier Reef. Although the organism may be seen by the naked eye, electron microscopic and genetic studies classify it as a bacterium.

blood. Some microorganisms produce disease in plants and animals. A fungus was responsible for the terrible potato famine in nineteenth-century Ireland, yet penicillin came from another type of fungus. Pathogens — disease-producing bacteria — grow best at body temperature. But there are some microorganisms that can live in glacial streams and some that even exist in hot springs.

Bacteria are one-cell organisms that generally reproduce asexually. Those that are spheres are named cocci. Straight rods are called bacilli and curved rods spirillae. The *rickettsiae* and *chlamydiae* are much smaller than other bacteria and can reproduce only inside the cells of host organisms.

Fungi are generally larger than bacteria and are commonly composed of more than one cell. They are subdivided into molds and yeasts.

Viruses are too small to be seen with the ordinary light microscope, and require the electron microscope which provides final magnifications of up to one million times The light microscope can magnify an image only about 1,000 times. Viruses do not grow on the synthetic media, so useful with bacteria, and do not reproduce themselves as bacteria do; rather they can only be reproduced within the living cells of their host. In other words, they subvert the cells they parasitize to perform the task for them.

Protozoa are relatively large, single-celled organisms that may have complex life cycles. Among the protozoa are the organisms responsible for malaria, sleeping sickness, and amoebic dysentery.

At first, Pasteur depended largely on his microscope for identifying microorganisms. He was extremely skilled as a morphologist, but, of course, his microscope could not bring into view all types of organisms. Besides that, he used unstained preparations, which are difficult to see. (Staining and the use of the oil immersion lens to attain greater magnification and higher resolution were adopted by his laboratory in 1884.) Nevertheless, his superb intuition convinced him of the existence of viruses, even if he could not see them. In 1885, he made this statement: "One is tempted to believe there is a microorganism infinitely small." Previously he had noted "the infinitely great power of the infinitely small."

To learn more about microbial action and to provide increased samples when organisms were sparse in his preparations, Pasteur multiplied organisms by growing them in a nutritive broth. In such a liquid medium, some organisms grow well, but if a mixture of organisms is present, separation of different types is very difficult. And the culture must be pure (all generations must be descendants of the same organism) if any reliable information is to be obtained. Transfer of a culture to a sterile growth medium was made with sterile glass pipettes. (By 1886, Pasteur's laboratory was using the platinum wire loop, which can be immediately sterilized in a flame, and which became standard equipment of the microbiologist.)

Pasteur was faced with another problem which would take time to be recognized: many organisms required special conditions to multiply. For example, molds grow best at temperatures lower than that optimum for bacteria, and in a more acidic medium; some bacteria, such as the one that causes tetanus (lockjaw), will not grow unless oxygen is excluded. Numerous unique growth requirements have been discovered over the years.

Neither crude microscopes nor unknown growth requirements were going to deter Pasteur. Later on, he often told students that his work on silkworms was good preparation for whatever veterinary or medical investigation was at hand. He was also fond of stating that the germ theory of fermentation was the foundation for his work on contagious disease. So, according to his own declaration, his previous successful approach to scientific problems had provided excellent preparation for the problems ahead.

The first problem to confront him involved a disease known as anthrax that primarily affects herbivorous animals, although man is susceptible. It is caused by a large bacillus, *Bacillus anthracis*. This was seen in 1850 by Casmir Davaine, a French physician-zoologist, and Pierre Olive, physician to Louis Philippe. They found the bacterium in the blood of a sheep that succumbed to anthrax. They also succeeded in producing that disease in one animal by inoculating it with blood from another infected animal. Davaine resolved to "find out whether the development of microscopically small creatures was not the cause of . . . the death of the animal." Thirteen years would pass before he had opportunity to do so.

An 1861 publication of Pasteur's dealing with the production of butyric acid by fermentation further whetted Davaine's interest. Two years later he had studied the anthrax bacillus enough to write: "The real agent is indeed visible and can be perceived; it is an organism, a living creature, which develops and is propagated as are living things.

Its presence and its rapid multiplication in the blood . . . cause rapid death of the infected animal."

Here we have a glimpse of the wonderment caused by the idea of microscopic life having the capability to destroy an animal as large as a cow. It helps us to understand why a generation that accepted the belief that a transmissible disease could arise from noxious air was reluctant to accept the germ theory of disease.

Davaine's finding was rejected by workers who could not find the bacilli he described in the blood of animals afflicted with anthrax. Fortunately the whole problem was soon investigated by Robert Koch, a German physician who would become as well known in bacteriology as Pasteur himself.

Koch grew the bacillus in cattle blood and aqueous humor, and was able to produce the disease in animals inoculated with his cultures. He also showed that animals became infected from the soil by way of their food. His very thorough study included the effects of moisture, temperature, and air on the organism. In working out the bacterium's life cycle, he proved a very important point: under certain conditions, spore formation took place in the blood and tissues of an animal killed by anthrax. While the bacilli themselves have relatively short lives, the spores that are formed can withstand prolonged drying and remain infective for years. Koch also distinguished the anthrax bacillus from the hay bacillus, a spore former that resembles it, but is not pathogenic. His results were published in 1876. Elegant as the work was, it still failed to impress some scientists.

As early as 1836, an Italian named Agostino Bassi had shown that a fungus was the cause of muscardine, one of the silkworm diseases, but his findings had little impact, for such a concept was too new.

With widespread doubt and misunderstanding about anthrax, and because it was causing great loss to French agriculture, Pasteur undertook to study the problem in 1877, enlisting the help of a former student named Jules François Joubert.

Pasteur quickly substantiated the claim that the anthrax bacillus was the agent causing the disease. He also showed that animals contracted the disease by eating grass that had become infected from the carcasses of buried animals; earthworms carried the organisms to the surface. He discovered that animals surviving the disease could not be reinfected — they were what we now call immune.

Pasteur thus reinforced Koch. This, of course, aided acceptance of the new theory, but Pasteur's major contribution to anthrax control revolves around immunology. He was 60 years old, and did not have too many years left, when he began to concentrate on the idea of immunization by means of specific vaccines for specific diseases. To appreciate the sequence of events, we must consider another veterinary disease — chicken cholera.

In 1878, a veterinary surgeon in Toulouse contacted Pasteur about this scourge, at the time causing great damage in French farm yards. Pasteur read the literature available to him and set out to isolate the organism believed to be responsible — it had been studied and reported by others. He devised a medium suitable for its growth and then injected the cultured organisms into animals to see the effects produced. He found that the adult guinea pig developed a local abscess, not the systemic disease seen in the chicken and rabbit. Nevertheless, the guinea pig could constitute a reservoir of infection for a more susceptible species; in other words, it was what we today call a carrier.

Pasteur was familiar with Jenner's work on the smallpox vaccination* and he had seen that animals who survived anthrax were immune. He now set out to "enfeeble" the bacterial culture so that injections of it would actually protect animals against chicken cholera.

It was only when Pasteur's laboratory notebooks were donated to the National Library in Paris in 1979 that the details of how he did this became more clear. He ultimately found that leaving the organisms in a weakly acidic medium for a long period of time would produce a culture weak enough not to kill and yet capable of inducing an immunity against a later injection of virulent organisms. In other words, he could immunize animals against chicken cholera by vaccination.

The immediate problem was to provide a reproducible method that would attenuate (weaken) anthrax bacillus in the same manner as he had attenuated the chicken cholera organism. Much of the work

*In 1798, Edward Jenner had shown that inoculation with pus from cowpox, a relatively benign disease, would protect against smallpox, a devastating one.

was of necessity done in the field. He had for this the assistance of Pierre Emile Roux and Charles Edouard Chamberland, each destined to become a famous bacteriologist in his own right.

According to Dubos, attenuation was at first produced by the addition of antiseptics. Later it was found by trial and error that by keeping the anthrax organisms for a week in neutral chicken bouillon maintained at 42°C (107°F), virulence for the guinea pig, sheep, and rabbit was lost. By appropriate selection of cultures with varying virulence, one could be found that would cause a mild form of anthrax. After recovery, the injected animals would produce sufficient antibodies to be immune to anthrax. Pasteur also found that rapid passage through animals would restore the virulence of attenuated cultures.

On May 5, 1881, he began one of the most colorful experiments known to science. At the instigation of an unconvinced veterinarian, the Melun Agricultural Society sponsored a project to demonstrate publicly whether or not Pasteur's vaccination method was valid, and supplied livestock for the experiment.

Pasteur arranged to inoculate 24 sheep, one goat, and six cows with the anthrax vaccine; later these same animals would be injected with a virulent anthrax culture. As controls he used 24 unvaccinated sheep, one unvaccinated goat, and four unvaccinated cows which would also be injected with the virulent culture. The vaccinated animals were expected to survive and the unvaccinated animals were expected to die of anthrax. When Roux and Chamberland expressed concern about getting perfect results, their chief remarked confidently, "What succeeded with 14 sheep in the laboratory will succeed with 50 in Melun."

The event, which took place at the farm of Pouilly le Fort, was highly publicized; in fact, M. de Blowitz, the Paris correspondent of the *London Times*, was present to write about it. Farmers, veterinarians and physicians watched with interest, some expecting — perhaps hoping — to see Pasteur fail. He was, after all, a professor and an outsider to their fields. The first vaccinations done on May 5 were followed by a second series on May 17. The crucial test inoculations of virulent organisms were made on May 31, with June 2 set as the date to determine whether the professor was right or wrong.

On June 2, Pasteur arrived, displaying his usual enthusiasm, at the field where the animals were on display. Accompanying him were Roux and Chamberland and another assistant, Louis Ferdinand Thuiller, who would later die in Egypt while investigating cholera.

According to Roux, "In the multitude at Pouilly le Fort, that day, there were no longer any skeptics, but only admirers." All the vaccinated sheep and cows were in good shape; 21 of the unvaccinated sheep and one goat had died of anthrax; the remaining unprotected sheep and cows were sick.

This success created a great demand for the anthrax vaccine, and its preparation was put under the supervision of Chamberland. Profits from sales in France were turned over to Pasteur's laboratory; profits from foreign sales went to Pasteur and his collaborators.

Not all the vaccine released was effective; some was contaminated with other organisms, some caused anthrax and some failed to protect against anthrax. It is now accepted that if the process were carried out exactly as recommended by Pasteur, protection was adequate for a limited period of time. It was soon found, however, that complete immunity could be maintained with annual vaccination.

Since that day at Pouilly le Fort, there has been reasonable expectation for the development of a vaccine once the causative organism is known. It is this expectation which today sustains the researchers working to find an effective AIDS vaccine.

Apart from Pasteur, there was other progress being made in bacteriology.

Pasteur's German counterpart of sorts was Robert Koch, mentioned in conjunction with anthrax. Pasteur's junior by some 20 years, Koch made many highly significant contributions.

The year 1872 saw Koch become district medical officer in a small town in Polish Prussia. At that time, he began to do bacteriological research in his own home. During his days as a student at Göttingen University, bacteriology, of course, was not part of the curriculum. But he had been greatly influenced by the teachings of the anatomist Jacob Henle, who believed in the infectious nature of disease. Koch's lab equipment included a good microscope and an incubator. He also set up to do microphotography and outfitted a small darkroom.

Within four years he had published his classical paper on anthrax. His next paper described techniques for fixing bacteria to glass slides, for staining them with aniline dyes, and for photographing them.

Figure 3-2 — Robert Koch, 1843-1910.
(Courtesy National Library of Medicine)

Stained, compared to unstained, bacteria are much easier to study, and Koch modified a staining method of Carl Weigert in Breslau. Dyes such as methylene blue, fuchsin, bismarck brown, and methyl violet came to be used.

A great advance was made in 1884 when a Danish physician named Hans Christian Joachim Gram published a method for differential staining. This provided a way to classify bacteria as gram-positive (the organisms retain a blue-violet dye) or gram-negative (the organisms counterstain with a red dye). For example, a coccus that causes pneumonia is gram-positive, and a coccus that causes meningitis is gram-negative. Gram staining is still important in microscopic diagnosis.

While investigating sepsis, Koch reiterated a fundamental idea of Henle: proof that the specific agent causing a given disease must be demonstrated by (1) its constant presence in the lesions, (2) isolation of this agent, and (3) reproduction of the disease by inoculation of this agent. This concept was expanded to become Koch's Postulates, familiar to the modern microbiologist.

Koch's work had gained him a reputation, and in 1880, he secured an appointment in Berlin with the Imperial Department of Health. His main assignment was to develop reliable methods for isolating and cultivating pathogenic bacteria and to gather bacterio-logic data and establish scientific principles related to hygiene and public health.

Koch developed solid media, an accomplishment that should not be underestimated. Both liquid and solid media have advantages, but a solid medium is almost indispensable in obtaining a pure culture from a mixture of organisms. Koch tried gelatin at first, then, following the suggestion of a colleague's wife, he added agar-agar (a gelatinous colloid extracted from a red alga which was used as a gelling agent in foods) to his growth medium to give it the consisten-cy of Jell-0™. The result was so successful that agar plates — Petri dishes containing sterilized culture medium with agar (figure 3-3) — are in common use in today's microbiology laboratory. Here is how such a plate is used.

Suppose it is necessary to know what bacterium (if any) is causing a child's sore throat. The throat's normal flora consists of many types of organisms, and the culprit must be differentiated quickly from these non-pathogenic organisms if treatment is to be

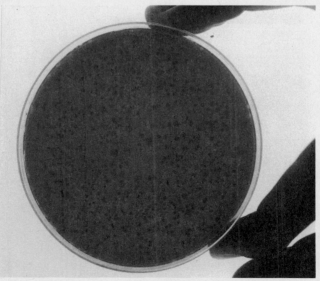

Figure 3-3 — Bacterial colonies on an agar plate.
(Courtesy Difco Corporation)

effective. A swab is passed over the reddened area in the throat and then streaked onto the surface of the medium. The covered Petri dish is placed in an incubator which maintains the sample at body temperature. If the correct nutritional factors are present, and, if other conditions are observed, usually within 24 hours, each bacterial organism present on the swab will have multiplied (by dividing into two parts; each of the two parts in turn dividing into two parts, etc.) to form what is called a colony, now visible to the eye. The appearance of such a colony, composed of millions of descendents of the original bacterium, helps to identify it. To complete the identification, various other tests are done, using organisms from the colony.

Research performed in this century has contributed immeasurably to making possible rapid identification of organisms without culturing them. Using direct immunologic methods, it is now often possible to determine the causative organism in less than 24 hours. To illustrate, rapid diagnosis of group A streptococcus, responsible in the pre-penicillin era for damage to the mitral valve of the heart, is available in even small labs. (A do-it-yourself, home test for the same organism is also popular.) Certain techniques of molecular biology hold great promise for routine laboratory use. Nevertheless, separating colonies on a solid medium remains a basic and reference technique of microbiology, and without pure cultures, results are often worthless. There has been some interest in the use of pectin, a product of certain fruits, as a solidifying agent.

When Koch attended the 1881 International Medical Congress in London, he demonstrated his pure-culture techniques in Lord Lister's laboratory. There he met Pasteur, who termed Koch's methods "a great improvement." Ironically, there would be unpleasant exchanges between the two in the future, for personal jealousies seem to have been aggravated by national pride.

Soon afterward, Koch began investigations of tuberculosis, a disease he believed to be infectious. This was an especially difficult task. We now know that the causative organism does not stain by ordinary methods. Fortunately Paul Ehrlich soon devised a way – the acid-fast stain. (He would attain fame as the father of chemotherapy for finding a drug to treat syphilis.) A second difficulty was the fastidious growth requirements of the bacterium; even when these were recognized, the growth was slow. Despite all this, by 1882,

Koch had isolated the tubercle bacillus and proved conclusively that it was the cause of the disease.

Today, it is difficult to realize the mortality and morbidity caused by tuberculosis. Frank Ryan's excellent book, *The Forgotten Plague*, emphasizes this. With its contagious nature established, much prevention was possible through the institution of hygienic measures. This work of Koch's was truly a banner event in the field of bacteriology.

While his brilliant proteges were working on other diseases, Koch studied tuberculin, a substance obtained from tubercle bacilli. Although tuberculin lacked the immunizing activity he ascribed to it, it proved useful in skin-testing for tuberculosis. (A drug active against the tubercle bacillus was not known until 1944.) Koch made another serious error in contending that bovine tuberculosis could not be transmitted to man. The British Royal Commission on Tuberculosis, appointed in 1911, proved him wrong. Nevertheless, Koch remains an outstanding figure in bacteriology and public health.

The researches first of Pasteur and then of Koch spurred attempts by others to find causative organisms of human diseases. Koch himself isolated the organism responsible for cholera. By 1894, a bacillus was known to cause typhoid fever; the bacillus responsible for diphtheria had been isolated; the presence of the staphylococcus had been correlated with suppurative wounds, abscesses, and the like; another coccus, the streptococcus, was known to be present in some septicemias and infections. Two years later, it was shown that the *Streptococcus pneumoniae* can cause lobar pneumonia. In 1887, still another coccus, the meningococcus, was proven to be the cause of spinal meningitis.

The term, Golden Age of Bacteriology, refers to the years 1880-1900 because so many advances were made (see table 3-1). Scourges such as cholera and plague that had ravaged and terrified man since ancient times were now better understood. At last there was proof of a causal relationship between certain microorganisms and certain diseases. However, as we shall see in the next chapter, there was considerable reluctance to accept this viewpoint. Overcoming this reluctance was perhaps the greatest of Pasteur's triumphs.

The modern microbiology laboratory is vastly different from that of Pasteur and Koch, although there is evidence of the lasting influence of some of their basic tenets. New diseases are discovered

Table 3-1

Discovery of Some Human Pathogens

Causative organism	Date
Trichinosis	1860
Amebic dysentery	1875
Gonorrhea	1879
Typhoid fever	1880
Leprosy	1880
Malaria	1880
Tuberculosis	1882
Cholera	1883
Erysipelas	1883
Diphtheria	1884
Tetanus	1884
Pneumonia (pneumococcus)	1884
Meningitis (meningococcus)	1887
Undulant fever	1887
Soft chancre	1989
Gas gangrene	1892
Botulism	1894
Plague	1894
Bacillary dysentery	1898
African sleeping sickness	1901
Yellow fever	1901
Syphilis	1905
Whooping cough	1906
Poliomyelitis	1908
Typhus (epidemic)	1916
Influenza	1933
Hepatitis B	1965
Legionnaire's disease*	1977
Human T-cell leukemia/lymphoma	1978
AIDS	1983
Lyme disease	1983

*First isolated in 1947, but pathogenicity largely unrecognized.

and gain prominence, more recent examples being Legionnaire's disease *(Legionella pneumophilia)* and AIDS (human immunodeficiency virus). AIDS is an acronym for acquired immunodeficiency syndrome.

Lyme disease *(Borellia burgdorferi)* is becoming familiar, and *Helicobacter pylori* is now recognized as a cause of gastritis and peptic ulcers and possibly of gastric carcinoma. Toxic shock syndrome is considered a new disease, but the causative organism is the familiar *Staphylococcus aureus. Chlamydia trachomatis,* a bacterium, has long been known as a cause of blindness in developing countries; in the United States it has become one of the most prevalent pathogens to be transmitted sexually.

Ever since penicillin became available, pharmaceutical companies have continued to introduce new antibiotics, creating, in turn, demand for corresponding antibiotic sensitivity tests to determine whether or not a given drug will inhibit the pathogen's growth. A new disease, antibiotic-associated pseudomembranous colitis, is due to a bacterium named *Clostridium difficile.*

Patients with AIDS, those with transplanted organs, and those with malignant disease have shown that organisms formerly considered of no great significance can cause death when the immune system is compromised. This condition may occur naturally or may be due to the use of immunosuppressive drugs or to a combination of the two. The organisms include sporozoan parasites such as

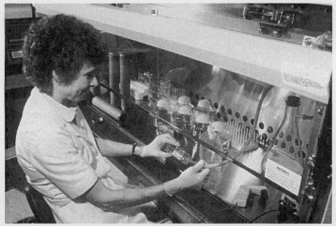

Figure 3-4 – Processing cell cultures in a modern biosafety cabinet.
(Courtesy Centers for Desease Control and Prevention)

Cryptosporidium, *Pneumocystis carinii*, and *Toxoplasma gondii;* also nontuberculous mycobacteria such as *Mycobacterium aviumintracellulare*; viruses such as that of herpes simplex, papillomavirus and cytomegalovirus; fungi such as *Cryptococcus neoformans.* Not so long ago, many of the foregoing names were seen only in technical literature. Now they are appearing in newspapers and popular magazines. We shall have more to say on this subject in Chapter 12.

Of course, automation and computers have had great impact. In large medical centers, especially, assembly-line methods are used to facilitate and speed up the diagnosis of microbial disease.

Change demands continuing assessment of laboratory methodology and services, so in all probability the microbiology laboratory of the twenty-first century will have little resemblance to that familiar in the 1990's.

Chapter 4

ACCEPTING THE INFINITELY SMALL

Pasteur was elected a member of the Academy of Medicine in 1873. An outsider to the profession, he was not trusted by some of its members, which included veterinarians. The importance of the latter should not be underestimated; scientist-writer W. I. B. Beveridge, in his 1977 book entitled *Influenza. The Last Great Plague*, noted that fungi, protozoa, mycoplasma, and viruses were first found to be the causes of disease in animals and only subsequently were shown to cause disease in man. In the 1990's, there is some concern about the spread of mad cow disease, more scientifically named bovine spongiform encephalopathy. So far, there is so evidence that it affects humans.

Some who opposed Pasteur must have wished they had not. One such was M. Colin, Professor at Alfort, who had studied anthrax for 12 years. He disputed the bacterial origin of the disease, arguing that some other organic matter in the blood was responsible. For months he continued his criticism.

Pasteur and his assistants Joubert and Chamberland had found that hens did not contract anthrax at their usual body temperature of lll°F (42°C), which is higher than that of susceptible animals. (Jules François Joubert later became a physician with a special interest in electricity. The Chamberland filter known to microbiologists was named for Charles Edouard Chamberland who invented it in 1884. He was also one of the earliest users of the autoclave.)

When Pasteur refuted Colin's statement that nothing was easier than to give the disease to hens, Colin said he would produce a hen with anthrax. But even with an active culture provided by Pasteur, Colin failed to back up his claim. To the Academy he reported: "I regret that I have not until now been able to hand to M. Pasteur a hen dying or dead of anthrax. The two that I had bought for that purpose were inoculated several times with very active blood, but neither of them has fallen ill. Perhaps the experiment might have succeeded afterwards, but one fine day, a greedy dog prevented that by eating up the two birds, whose cage had probably been badly closed."

But Pasteur would not let the matter rest there. A few days later, he arrived at the Academy of Medicine with a cage containing two live hens, one gray and one black, plus a white one, which was dead. He said the latter had died 29 hours after inoculation with a pure culture of anthrax bacilli. He explained that the animal's body temperature had been lowered by placing the hen in a water bath at 100°F (38°C). The uninoculated gray hen was a control; it had been immersed under identical conditions, but recovered quickly. The black hen — lively and apparently in good health — had been inoculated at the same time as the white one, and with twice the amount of the same culture, but it had not been put into the bath, therefore maintaining at all times its regular body temperature. Pasteur made it clear that, without exception, hens treated similarly to the white one had died with typical anthrax and that anthrax bacilli had been found in their blood, spleen, lungs, and liver. It is likely that after that, no member of the Academy was inclined to defend Colin's argument.

That Pasteur realized the difficulty of his position is shown in what he wrote to a veterinarian who was a member of the Academy of Sciences. Pasteur acknowledged his ignorance of some medical and veterinary matters, but made it clear that his conclusions relating to these fields were backed up with strong proofs.

In 1880, he was speaking on vaccination to the Academy of Medicine when he was refuted by the 80-year-old Jules Guérin, a surgeon. Angry, Pasteur ridiculed some operating procedures practiced by Guérin. The older man became incensed and rushed to strike Pasteur. A colleague interceded, but the next day Guérin sent two seconds to challenge Pasteur to a duel. Pasteur backed down enough to satisfy the octogenarian – and put his words into writing.

The episode shows something of the atmosphere that existed. A medical journal of the day commented:

> We, for our part, admire the meekness of M. Pasteur, who is so often described as combative and ever on the warpath. Here we have a scientist, who now and then makes short, substantial, and extremely interesting communications. He is not a medical man, and yet, guided by his genius, he opens new paths across the most arduous of medical science. Instead of being offered the tribute of attention and admiration which he deserves, he meets with a raging apposition from some quarrelsome individuals, ever inclined to contradict after listening as little as possible. If he makes use of a scientific expression not understood by everyone, or if he uses a medical expression slightly incorrectly, then rises before him the spectre of endless speeches, intended to prove to him that all was for the best in medical science before it was assisted by the precise studies and resources of chemistry and experimentation . . . .

Determined to learn everything he could about human diseases, Pasteur frequently visited hospital clinics and morgues in the company of Roux and Chamberland, the latter two armed with equipment necessary for taking cultures. (Due to the permanent paralysis, Pasteur was severely limited in physical activity.) Although ill at ease on the wards, through such visits he became convinced that what we now call *Streptococcus pyogenes* was the agent that causes puerperal fever. When he cultured pus from a boil on the skin of his assistant Duclaux, he found the organism now known as *Staphylococcus aureus*. Later, when he noticed the same coccus present in a case of osteomyelitis, he termed the condition "boil of the bone." Peculiar as the terminology is, he was correct. If some members of the Academy of Medicine were dubious about Pasteur's findings with regard to anthrax, which is essentially an animal disease, it is not surprising that they were cautious about accepting what he said about the microbial origins of some human diseases.

Great epidemics, as well as the spread, though less spectacular, of some diseases made the concept of contagion believable. The problem was the acceptance of the thesis that unseen forms of life were capable of invading the body, multiplying there, and in so doing, causing devastation such as a fatal septicemia – or in layman's parlance, blood poisoning.

For years, the miasma theory had been popular. This held that contagion was due to putrid emanations from corpses or other rotting material. Such an idea was dispelled, or should have been, by what is elegantly called the Great Stench of London, which occurred in 1858. Due to an exceptionally hot summer, the sewage dumped into the River Thames produced an odor that threatened to shut down that great city. It penetrated the Houses of Parliament and caused law courts to close down and river steamers to lose their passengers. But despite such unpleasantness, *the death rate for the period was below average and there was a significant decline in cases of fever, diarrhea, and other maladies usually attributed to miasma.*

Among the scientists and physicians receptive to the germ theory was Jacob Henle. In 1840, he had expressed the belief that living parasitic agents probably caused infectious disease. Four years later, Bassi, whom we mentioned in connection with silkworm disease, stated that "smallpox, spotted fever, bubonic plague, and syphilis are caused by living parasites, animal and vegetable."

Some who rejected the miasma theory in favor of the germ theory, however, believed in pleomorphism – the theory that bacteria could transform themselves into different types. To add to the confusion, individual diseases were often misdiagnosed clinically, one being mistaken for another. (It was 1817 before typhus was differentiated from typhoid fever. Credit for this goes to physician William G. Garland of Philadelphia.)

An early believer in the germ theory, and one of the most influential, was Joseph Lister. At 33, Lister was appointed professor of clinical surgery at the Royal Infirmary in Glasgow. The year was 1860, and hospitals were known as breeding places of infection; erysipelas, hospital gangrene, and suppuration were considered inevitable in the patients. Patients might survive surgery, but die later of septicemia. Opening the abdomen was seldom attempted because the risk of peritonitis was so great. Although ether anesthesia had been introduced in 1846, its full benefit could not be realized until

Figure 4-1 — Joseph Lister, 1827-1912
(Courtesy National Library of Medicine)

infection was under control. Sir James Simpson of chloroform anesthesia fame asserted that "the man laid on the operating-table in one of our surgical hospitals is exposed to more chances of death than the English soldier on the field of Waterloo." It is small wonder that such conditions existed; the state of knowledge was such that it was not unusual for the surgeon to put the suturing thread into his mouth before inserting it into the needle's eye.

Lister himself was losing 45 percent of his amputation cases to infection. He noticed that compound fractures, with the overlying skin broken, almost always produced suppuration. On the other hand, simple fractures, with the skin and surrounding tissues undamaged, healed without infection. Disturbed by the situation at hand, he tried to solve the problem of sepsis. Years would elapse before he was successful. But successful he was, thanks to his native ability and Pasteur's publications on fermentation.

Lister was well equipped to do research. He had already done some original investigation in physiology and was well versed in microscopy. The latter interest was due to his father, whose discoveries greatly improved achromatic lenses for microscopes and other optical instruments. In 1865, through Thomas Anderson, Professor of Chemistry at the university, Lister became acquainted with Pasteur's contention that fermentation and putrefaction were related, both being due to microorganisms in the air. In view of his clinical knowledge, Lister became convinced that infection was due to microorganisms and that keeping the air out of a wound would prevent infection.

Since carbolic acid (phenol) had been used for the disinfection of sewage at Carlisle, Lister decided to try it for compound fractures. He was unaware that two years earlier a Frenchman named Jules Lemaire had advocated the use of carbolic acid as a disinfectant.

A case presented itself in March, 1865. Lister packed the wound with lint soaked in a solution of crude carbolic acid, after washing it out with the same fluid. He then covered the dressing with a thin sheet of metal to prevent evaporation. The result was gratifying: the healing was good. Encouraged, he used this treatment on similar cases over the next two years. He also used the disinfectant in amputations and other operative wounds. In April, 1867, he wrote that "since the antiseptic treatment has been brought into full operation . . . my wards, though in other respects under precisely the same conditions as before, have completely changed their character, so that during the last nine months not a single instance of pyaemia, hospital gangrene, or erysipelas has occurred in them."

In 1870, Lister, then at Edinburgh University, had begun the unpopular technique of spraying the operating theater with a weak solution of carbolic acid. Phenol numbs the skin, sometimes causing severe burns. In addition, some people are hypersensitive to it. A letter from Lister to Pasteur dated 1874 said:

> "I do not know whether the records of British Surgery ever meet your eye. If so, you will have seen from time to time notices of the antiseptic system of treatment, which I have been laboring for the last nine years to bring to perfection.
>
> "Allow me to take this opportunity to tender you my most cordial thanks for having by your brilliant researches, demonstrated to me the truth of the germ theory of putrefaction, and thus furnished me with the

principle upon which alone the antiseptic system can be carried out."

Antisepsis was disliked by Lister's colleagues, but some surgeons on the European continent were more receptive. Among these were Theodore Billroth of Vienna, one of the outstanding surgeons of the day. (He also embraced the incorrect pleomorphism theory.) Antisepsis would ultimately give way to asepsis, but since phenol had proved so effective, it did much to promote belief in the germ theory. Ironically, excluding air from wounds encourages the growth of anaerobic spore formers such as that of the bacilli that cause tetanus and gas gangrene. Of course, Lister did not know this until after the discovery of these organisms.

At first, Pasteur remained a prophet without honor in his own country; French surgeons were not convinced. However, toward the end of the Franco-Prussian War, one surgeon, Alphonse Guérin, became a convert to the idea that Pasteur's "living corpuscles" might be a source of infection. By using antiseptics and keeping the wounds covered for about three weeks, he began to save lives, much to the amazement of his fellow physicians.

While Lister emphasized the presence of bacteria in the air, Pasteur's observations in the wards prompted the belief that bacteria were introduced into wounds mainly by hospital personnel. To the Academy of Medicine he mentioned, "the invasion of these infinitely small organisms that, unwittingly, you have introduced into the wounded part." He advised asepsis, a preventive technique to avoid the introduction of organisms. This entailed the use of bandages and sponges previously exposed to a temperature high enough to kill bacteria. He advocated hand washing and even passing the hands rapidly through a flame to destroy the organisms normally present on the skin.

Antisepsis worked for Lister because phenol is bactericidal. He seemed less concerned with contamination coming from human beings than with contamination from the air. In either case, antisepsis cut down the frequency of infections. Asepsis, which had a better theoretical basis and was more practical, gradually gained prominence. One of its chief promoters was Ernest von Bergmann, who, in 1882, became Professor of Surgery at the University of Berlin. Four years later, he introduced steam sterilization and by 1891 was employing asepsis. In the same country, Koch investigated wound infections, publishing a book on the subject in 1887. In it he described six different bacteria that infected wounds and the effects produced by each. Octave Terrillon of Paris was another French surgeon who supported Pasteur's views and put them into effect.

Earlier, we mentioned the high maternal death rate in Paris hospitals. Pasteur knew that the streptococcus causing puerperal fever could be carried by attendants from a patient with a wound infection to one who had just delivered. This disease was the scourge of every maternity hospital and the terror of poor women who had to use them.

Warnings about puerperal fever antedated Pasteur. As early as 1820, Robert Collins of Dublin's Rotunda Hospital was controlling the disease by using the French method of fumigation with chlorine. He also ordered heat sterilization of bed linens and blankets. His methods met with success. Yet after he left that hospital, his technique was abandoned.

In the United States, Oliver Wendell Holmes Sr. published *Contagiousness of Puerperal Fever* in 1843. In this he implicated physicians.

Four years later in Vienna, the Hungarian Ignaz Semmelweiss concluded from autopsy reports that, in one clinic, puerperal fever was transmitted mainly by the hands of doctors and medical students who had come from postmortem examinations. The next year, Semmelweiss demanded that all who examined maternity patients routinely wash their hands in a solution of calcium hypochlorite. This resulted in a sharp drop in deaths from puerperal fever.

Few in the medical profession took either Holmes or Semmelweiss seriously. But Pasteur, secure in his knowledge of the specific organism and possessing a fighting spirit that asserted itself when he had a mission, eventually convinced the reluctant doctors to change their ways.

Pasteur's past accomplishments, his scholarship and his personality all contributed to his success in bringing veterinarians and physicians to a general acceptance of the germ theory of disease.

Pasteur once said, "When meditating over a disease, I never think of a remedy for it but, instead, a means of preventing it." This is the basic philosophy of the science of public health, a science that came into its own once the germ theory of disease became part of people's thinking.

As enlightenment spread during the nineteenth century, there were some improvements in water supplies, sanitation, general hygiene, and cleanliness. Such empirical action did much to cut down microbial contamination, as Florence Nightingale so convincingly showed. During the Crimean War, the sanitary measures that she instituted were responsible for drastic reduction in the mortality of British soldiers dying from infectious disease. Ironically, this able and heroic woman did not believe in the germ theory of disease.

British physician John Snow had shown that cholera could be transmitted from person to person and also by ingestion of infected food and water. It would be some 30 years before Koch isolated *Vibrio cholerae,* the bacteria responsible for the disease. Snow pointed out that excreta from cholera patients could pollute wells and thereby aid in the spread of the disease. His contemporary, William Budd, recognized that typhoid could be transmitted by contaminated water. Findings such as these made some people more willing to give credence to the belief that specific agents could cause specific maladies.

There were gaps and puzzles in the germ theory, but they were elucidated in a relatively short time. The carrier state was not recognized immediately. It was clear enough that a person who was acutely ill with diphtheria could pass on the disease to another person. However, well and convalescent people might harbor diphtheria bacilli in their throats. In 1894, William Park and Alfred Beebe of New York City's Health Department clearly established this. It was found that carriers play a role in the dissemination of other diseases — cholera, typhoid, spinal meningitis, poliomyelitis, and dysentery.

Recognition of vectors came gradually, although, in 1790, a Danish physician-veterinarian named Peter Christian Abilgaard had found that parasites may pass through stages in their life cycles in animals other than those species which they normally infect. *Trypanosoma evansi* is the causative organism of surra, a parasitic disease of horses. Surra is similar to sleeping sickness in man. Griffith Evans, a British physician-veterinarian serving in India, discovered in sick horses what was later named *Trypanosoma evansi.* He then succeeded in producing the disease in well horses by injecting them with blood from sick horses. He was also able to transmit surra to a dog whose blood then showed the organisms. *(The Several Lives of a Victorian Vet* is a fascinating account of Griffith Evans' life.)

Evans could not convince most of his scientific contemporaries that the parasites they could see in the blood from his sick horses were pathogenic. The year was 1880 and there was resistance to the germ theory of disease. But Evans himself was progressive. According to his diary: "I had kept myself informed of Pasteur's investigations and discoveries of pathogenic bacteria and was deeply impressed with the conviction that a new door was opening for great developments in medical science."

Evans' suggestion that the parasites were transferred from one horse to another by bloodsucking flies was also ignored at the time. However, 19 years later, Leonard Rogers showed that *Trypanosoma evansi* was indeed transferred by the bite of tabanid flies.

By 1897, there was significant information on malaria. That year, Ronald Ross, of the Indian Medical Service, found the parasites of human malaria in the stomach of an *Anopheles* mosquito. The following year, Ross experimentally transmitted avian malaria. His procedure was to have mosquitoes feed on birds infected with malaria and then have them bite healthy birds. Before Ross could show that human malaria was transmitted in the same manner, he was scooped by investigators in Rome. As Ross had surmised, malaria is usually transmitted by a female mosquito (of the genus *Anopheles)* that has picked up the causative organism *(Plasmodium,* a protozoan), which has a complex life cycle, from the blood of an infected person and transferred it to the blood of a healthy one through biting. Table 4-1 lists some vectors of human diseases caused by microorganisms.

In the latter half of the 19th century, the United States made considerable progress in public health. New York City, prompted by the fear of cholera, started the first city board of health in 1866. (Epidemic cholera has not occurred in the United States since 1873. However, it is an ever-present danger. During the 1990's, it raged in Peru, spread to Mexico, and continues today as a serious threat.) The first state board of health was established in Massachusetts in 1869. By 1908, Chicago had established compulsory pasteurization of milk. Gradually, there emerged local and state regulation of health matters concerning the public. Today, the United States Centers for Disease Control and Prevention (CDCP), formerly called the Centers for

Table 4-1

Dicovery of SomeVectors of Human Disease

Disease	Vector	Discovery
African sleeping sickness (cattle)	Tsetse fly	1894
Plague	Rat flea	1898
Malaria	Mosquito	1898
Yellow fever	Mosquito	1900
Dengue	Mosquito	1906
Rocky Mountain spotted fever	Wood tick	1906
Typhus (epidemic)	Body louse	1909
Colorado tick fever	Wood tick	1940
St. Louis encephalitis	Mosquito	1945
Lyme disease	Deer tick	1983

Disease Control (CDC), in Atlanta, has excellent resources for investigating and controlling outbreaks of infection.

On the international front, the World Health Organization (WHO), established in 1948 as a specialized agency of the United Nations, set out to bring the benefits of up-to-date scientific knowledge to less developed parts of the world, with the agreement and cooperation of the local governments involved. One of the outstanding accomplishments of WHO has been the eradication of smallpox. A laboratory accident in 1978 resulted in two cases and one death. But in 1977, a man in Ethiopia contracted the last naturally acquired case of smallpox. There is no animal reservoir in nature for this disease, a circumstance that aided eradication. Plans are in place to abolish polio and other childhood diseases for which there are preventive vaccines.

Chapter 5

VACCINES

By 1885, Pasteur had developed three vaccines important to agriculture: one for chicken cholera, one for anthrax, and one for swine erysipelas. The virulence of the organisms had been attenuated by different means. He was about to produce a vaccine to prevent rabies.

France now had a president; the liberal Gladstone had succeeded Disraeli as Prime Minister of Great Britain; Cleveland had replaced Arthur as the United States President; Mark Twain's *Huckleberry Finn* was enjoying great popularity; *The Mikado* made its debut; gold had been discovered in the Transvaal; London had an underground railway; canned fruits and meats were available in some stores. *Das Kapital* was about to be published in England and the Statue of Liberty to be dedicated in the United States.

Just why Pasteur chose rabies research is not clear. Today in the United States, nearly all dogs have been immunized against rabies and the human disease is almost nonexistent. The situation in Pasteur's day was more precarious, but cases of human rabies were relatively rare – in France, about 100 per annum. Whatever Pasteur's reasons, his selection of rabies was a master stroke from the standpoint of public relations. The thought of a person, perhaps a child, bitten by a rabid dog and then doomed to die an agonizing death, struck terror in the average mind. Certainly there was enormous appeal in the hope that a vaccine could ward off the dread symptoms; success with rabies would be a major step on the way to convincing the public that

Figure 5-1 — Pasteur with Mme. Pasteur - 1884 (Courtesy Pasteur Institute)

vaccination would be a valuable weapon to fight many diseases, not just smallpox.

Pasteur was aware that, in 1879, Victor Pierre Galtier of the Lyons Veterinary School had shown that by biting, a dog could transmit rabies to another animal, and that the infective agent, which was present in the saliva, was somehow spread along the nerves. He had also found that the rabbit was a good test animal for rabies and he had made some progress in immunization. He had not been able to transmit rabies consistently, which was a serious deficit in his work. Nevertheless, Galtier's studies gave Pasteur a good foundation for his proposed endeavor.

In December 1890, a young child died of rabies. Pasteur

obtained some of her saliva and injected it into a rabbit. The rabbit died in a short time, but not of rabies. Pasteur isolated from the saliva the organism that is now known as the pneumococcus – more scientifically as *Streptococcus pneumoniae*. He also soon realized that it was not the cause of rabies.

When his usual culture methods failed to produce the sought-for organism, infectious material was introduced into a dog's brain. This involved trephining the skull and it was done by Roux since Pasteur shrank from such a procedure. It was soon established that after inoculation by trephination, a dog consistently developed rabies in about 14 days. After several successive transfers of the disease from rabbit to rabbit, the inoculation period fell to 7 days.

This was a significant advance; a reproducible means of growing the agent responsible for rabies, now known to be a virus, had been found. The genius of Pasteur is apparent here. His *in vivo* method for culturing bacteria had been supplanted by an *in vitro* method. He could no longer depend on his microscope to show the presence of the organism, yet he knew that an "infinitely small" agent was present. He could demonstrate its presence by its action rather than its appearance. As usual, his confidence was based on excellent intuition, careful observation, and well-designed experiment.

Ordinarily, a preventive vaccine is given before exposure to a disease. Rabies presents a unique situation. Virus from the animal's saliva enters the victim's tissues when the animal bites. The organism then multiplies, remaining at first near the site of injury. Later it travels along peripheral nerves to enter the central nervous system, where it causes a characteristic and severe encephalitis that is almost always fatal. This may appear from 30 to 90 days after infection, depending on the distance of the wound from the brain. One of the distinguishing symptoms is hydrophobia, a choking or gagging sensation experienced when the patient tries to drink.

Pasteur intended to capitalize on the long incubation period. He believed that the vaccine could prevent the occurrence of rabies if administration were begun soon enough after the person was bitten. The problem at hand was to produce such an antirabies vaccine, a monumental task in light of the scant knowledge available. Undeterred, Pasteur forged ahead, though ailing and growing old.

By October 1885, progress was such that he could announce to the Academy of Science:

As a result of many experiments, so many as to be almost past counting, I have arrived at a quick, practical prophylactic method whose successes in the case of dogs have been so numerous and so consistent that I feel confident it can be applied to animals in general, and even to human beings.

The method developed consisted of a series of 7 to 14 daily injections of live, *attenuated* rabies virus in the form of dried spinal cord from rabies-injected rabbits.

Attenuation was accomplished by drying the infected spinal cords. (Most authorities believe that Roux contributed significantly to perfecting the attenuation technique.) Solutions of bouillon containing small pieces of dried cord were injected under the skin of the animal undergoing immunization. The injection schedule was so arranged that the longest dried — and therefore the least virulent — portions of cord were injected at the beginning of the series. With this regimen, there had been no failures in making 50 dogs resistant to rabies.

Monday, July 6, 1895 was a fateful day for Pasteur. Three people from Alsace arrived at his laboratory. One was a grocer whose dog had developed rabies. Another was Joseph Meister, age 9, whom the animal had bitten. The third person was Joseph's mother.

Here is Pasteur's own account of what happened:

The weekly session of the Academie des Sciences was due for that day, July 6; I attended it, and saw our colleague Dr. Vulpian, to whom I described what had happened. Dr. Vulpian and Professor Grancher of the Faculty of Medicine were kind enough to come and see little Joseph Meister at once and observe the number and nature of his wounds, of which there were no less than fourteen.

The opinion of our learned colleague and Dr. Grancher was that in view of the number and gravity of the bites Joseph Meister was almost certain to contract rabies . . . . I decided, not without acute and harrowing anxiety, as may be imagined, to apply to Joseph Meister that method which I had found consistently successful with dogs.

Pasteur's relief was expressed in this statement: "From the middle of August onward, I felt confident about the future of little Meister's health." He was convinced that, had the child not been immunized by the procedure, the later injections would have by themselves very soon produced rabies.

Meister was followed by a young shepherd from the Jura named Jean-Baptiste Jupille. This youth had been bitten as he tried to prevent a rabid dog from attacking some children. Six days later, on October 20, his inoculations were begun. His treatment again brought success.

As the word spread that there was available a treatment for rabies, more victims trooped to Pasteur's laboratory, among them 19 Russians bitten by rabid wolves, a Basque peasant, an Hungarian, and a British family.

More people bitten by rabid animals continued to arrive. According to Duclaux, "Laboratory and consultation room soon became too small; we had to leave the hospitable Rue d'Ulm to establish ourselves on larger grounds borrowed from the former Collège Rollin. It was while we camped there that the international subscription was opened which resulted in the creation of the Pasteur Institute."

By October 1886, 2,500 people had received the vaccine. Of course there were failures, especially among those who came too late. That made it popular to claim that the vaccine itself caused death. (It is now known that the vaccine could produce serious allergic reactions.)

Criticism of Pasteur began to mount. Again there was hostility from the medical profession. Dr. Jacques Joseph Grancher, who did the inoculations, described the situation. He related that one day when he went to the medical school, he heard a voice asserting that Pasteur was an assassin. When Grancher's colleagues recognized him, they walked away in silence. Antivivisectionists, medical and political journals, as well as politicians, joined the anti-Pasteur campaign; even Paris college students took sides over the issue.

Roux had resisted treating human rabies, but he came to Pasteur's defense when the Academy of Medicine attacked.

The objections of the medical community were similar to those which had been encountered in England by Jenner, despite the fact that he was one of them. He was forced into private publication because the Royal Society returned the manuscript that described his results on vaccination for smallpox. Today, medical historians rank Jenner's discovery among the greatest advances in the field of medicine.

The objections voiced to Pasteur's installation of kennels to house immunized animals is reminiscent of discontent that arose in a later day over nuclear power plants and genetic engineering. One letter from Pasteur stated,

> ". . . there will be no mad dogs at Villeneuve l'Etang, but only dogs made refractory to rabies. Not having enough room in my laboratory, I am actually obliged to quarter on various veterinary surgeons those dogs, which I should like to enclose in covered kennels, quite safely secured, you may be sure."

It has been shown repeatedly that, with Pasteur's rabies treatment, 99.5 percent of individuals bitten by rabid dogs survive. There is, however, some doubt about the efficacy of the method because the probability that a given exposed case will develop rabies is not known; as stated previously, this depends largely upon the depth and location of the bite.

Today, the first treatment of a wound likely to be infected with rabies virus is thorough washing with soap and water. Then, rabies immune globulin, a preparation of antibodies obtained from people immunized against rabies, is given. Half the dose is delivered directly into the wound, the remainder into the deltoid muscle. The vaccine in current use a century after Pasteur is more effective and safer than Pasteur's — a product of what is known as hybridoma technique. Veterinarians, personnel involved in bat research, and others in professions at risk generally receive the vaccine before engaging in pursuits where being bitten by a rabid animal is a possibility.

The criticism of Pasteur was countered by many both inside and outside the medical profession. In response to Pasteur's suggestion that "a vaccinal institute against hydrophobia" be established, the Academy of Sciences appointed a commission to study the matter. Following the successful treatment of the Meister boy, Edme Felix Alfred Vulpian, distinguished physician and Perpetual Secretary of the Academy, encouraged the idea.

Figure 5-2 – Original building of the Pasteur Institute. *(Courtesy O. Reynolds)*

The commission's recommendation was that private funds be sought within France and elsewhere for the creation of what was to be named the Institut Pasteur.

With great interest, Pasteur watched the construction of the buildings that would constitute the institute to be named in his honor. It would be a center not only for the treatment of rabies, but also for research on contagious diseases. ·Rich and poor alike had contributed to the enterprise. In addition to support from the French government, there had been international gifts. Sufficient funds had been collected for an endowment that would be added to each year by the income from the sale of vaccines, which Pasteur, Roux, and Chamberland agreed to donate to the endowment. (Later, Pasteur and his colleagues shared the profits from their patents in countries other than France.) The dedication of the Pasteur Institute took place on November 14, 1888.

In theory, Pasteur was its director, but his health had become so precarious that much of the administration fell to Duclaux. There were 15 physicians and scientists associated with the institute. Although Pasteur was in poor physical condition, his mind was very active and he took great intellectual interest and pride in the progress of the enterprise.

Elie Metchnikoff, a future Nobel Laureate, was at the Institute and was impressed that Pasteur still came to the laboratory and asked questions about work in progress, even though he was no longer capable of carrying on investigative work himself. Metchnikoff recalled that Pasteur never discouraged his students and collaborators; on the contrary, he wished to instill in them the same enthusiasm for science that he himself possessed.

On December 27, 1892, scientists representing many countries gathered in the amphitheater of the Sorbonne to celebrate Pasteur's seventieth birthday. As guest of honor, he was escorted by Sadi Carnot, President of the French Republic. There were tributes from the world's great, including Lister. Pasteur had his prepared speech read aloud by his son, for he was not up to delivering it himself.

Friends and admirers came to visit at the on-the-premises living quarters that were provided for the Pasteurs by the institute during the last six years of the scientist's life. One visitor was Pasteur's friend for longer than 50 years, Charles Chappuis, Honorary Rector at the Academy of Dijon.

Late in April 1895, Pasteur looked at microscopic organisms for the last time. He was carried to Roux's laboratory where he was shown the plague bacillus, discovered the year before. "Ah, what a lot there is still to do!" he said.

Death came on September 28, 1895. Pasteur lies in a chapel at what is now the Institute's Museum. Jean-Baptiste Pasteur had a hand in the design. On the walls are representations of his father's work: 1848, molecular dissymmetry; 1857, fermentations; 1862, spontaneous generation; 1863, studies of wine; 1865, silk worm diseases; 1871, studies of beer; 1877, infectious diseases; 1880, vaccines; 1885, prevention of rabies. He is guarded by four angels—Faith, Hope, Charity, and Science. Later Mme. Pasteur was buried in the same chapel. On the ceiling a mosaic of Jean-Baptiste Jupille struggling to ward off a rabid dog serves as another reminder of Pasteur's research.

Chapter 6

WEAKNESSES AND STRENGTHS

Being an outstanding scientist and adored by most of his countrymen does not confer perfection on Pasteur. His combative nature served to subdue his detractors, but occasionally he was in error, and sometimes he could have been more gracious to those who opposed him. Critics have pointed out that his disagreement with Claude Bernard's posthumous publication was not to his credit.

The illustrious Bernard had been on friendly professional terms with Pasteur. After Bernard's death in 1877, the chemist Marcellin Berthelot and others published some notes made by the physiologist. A few experiments on alcoholic fermentation apparently had led Bernard to conclude that fermentation could take place without the presence of yeast cells. This view refuted Pasteur, to whom it inferred the acceptance of spontaneous generation. Although Bernard could not defend himself, Pasteur lost no time in conveying to the Academy of Science his thoughts on this:

> On reading those opinions of Bernard, I experience both surprise and sorrow; surprise because the rigorous mind I used to admire in him is completely absent in this physiological mysticism; sorrow because our illustrious colleague seems to have forgotten the demonstrations which I have presented in the past. Have I not, for

example, carefully described as early as 1872, and more particularly in my Studies on Beer in 1876, a technique to extract grape juice from the inside of a berry, and to expose its juice in contact with pure air, and have I not shown that, under these conditions, yeast does not appear and ordinary fermentation does not take place? . . . It has also been painful to me to realize that all this was taking place under the auspices of our eminent colleague M. Berthelot.

To emphasize his position, Pasteur repeated, in extended form, some of his earlier experiments on fermentation.

At the heart of the controversy was Pasteur's insistence that alcoholic fermentation was a function of life, while Bernard regarded it as a chemical process. The latter view was held by Justus von Liebig, noted German chemist, by Swedish chemist Jons Jakob Berzelius, and by Berthelot. Berthelot had even found a substance in yeast which is now recognized as an enzyme capable of splitting cane sugar into two simple sugars.

As late as 1878, Pasteur had stated that he would not be at all surprised if yeast cells could produce a soluble alcoholic ferment. He also made the point that enzymes are always the products of life. ". . . the statement that fermentation is caused by an enzyme," he said, "does not contribute to our further understanding of the problem as long as no one has succeeded in separating the fermentation in an active form, free of living cells."

In 1897, in Germany, two brothers named Eduard and Hans Buchner showed that alcoholic fermentation could take place in the absence of the yeast cell – something that Pasteur had tried to demonstrate without success. As is now well established, the process is enzymatic. (In 1907, Eduard Buchner received a Nobel Prize for showing this.) The yeast cells that are present on the skin of the grape contain the necessary enzymes. Thus, the process is correctly termed either chemical or catalytic. Pasteur's opponents are vindicated and his own viewpoint appears narrow.

But Pasteur's reverence for the truth never deserted him. ". . . it has always been puzzling to me," he wrote, "why people imagined that I would be embarrassed by the discovery of soluble ferments . . . independent of cells." We should remember that he always contended that fermentation depended on microorganisms and that such organisms did not have spontaneous origin. It was his zeal to rid science of the concept of spontaneous generation that made him unreasonably stubborn and abusive to opponents such as Liebig. His mission was first to try "to convince myself . . . then to convince others . . . the third, probably less useful, but very enjoyable, which consists in convincing one's adversaries."

Liebig did not take Pasteur's criticism lightly. In an 1872 letter to Duclaux, he stated that he would not dream of attacking Pasteur's reputation — a fine reputation and one justly deserved. Nevertheless, he, Liebig, had only assigned a chemical cause to a chemical phenomenon.

Pasteur's remarks could be cutting, to say the least. He once said that M. Colin (page 45) was prone to look into 98 dark closets and to conclude from what he found that there was no light outside!

Pasteur had a distrust of the medical profession. He believed that physicians were inclined to engage in hasty generalizations. He allowed that they were endowed with a quick intelligence and were eager for knowledge. But with little time available for investigative work, they were prone to accept too readily inadequately proven theories — theories that were attractive to them.

Perhaps Pasteur's disputes with those who disagreed with him were beneficial; according to Roux, contention with members of the Academy of Medicine always spurred his chief to do further research.

Toward the end of his life, Pasteur defended his disputation by declaring that if he had sometimes disturbed the calm of the French Academies with somewhat violent discussions, it was because he was passionately defending truth.

"He wanted to be alone in his laboratory and never spoke of the goal he had in mind," recounted Adrien Loir, who was Pasteur's nephew and laboratory assistant during the years 1834-35. Duclaux gave the same story. When Pasteur was granted assistance from promising young scientists, he was not disposed to acquaint them with his goals and thoughts. Rather, he assigned specific tasks with the expectation that these would be carried out precisely as he directed.

This attitude caused some resentment on the part of his assistants, and it has been emphasized that Duclaux, when in position to do so, proceeded much differently. Dubos' book made it clear that

Duclaux wanted to make the new Pasteur Institute a cooperative research institution where the bright minds of France and, indeed, from around the globe could devote themselves to the advancement of biological and medical science – and in a state of complete independence.

In contrast to Duclaux's openness, Pasteur's secretive nature was less desirable in science. Why Pasteur chose to withhold his overall aims from his assistants is not known. As we have seen, Pasteur worked alone for some time. We do know that his work occupied him to such a degree that Mme. Pasteur wrote in 1884, "Your father is absorbed in his thoughts, talks little, sleeps little, rises at dawn, and, in one word, continues the life I began with him this day thirty-five years ago."

According to Pasteur himself, he was not one to rush into print without adequate data to back up his claims:

> To believe one has discovered an important scientific fact, to long to announce it, and yet to restrain oneself for days, weeks, sometimes even years; to strive to disprove one's own experiments; to publish one's discovery only after exhausting every alternative – yes, the task is a hard one. But when, after long endeavor, certainty is reached, the reward is one of the keenest joys of which the human soul is capable.

Apparently, not everyone was convinced that Pasteur always exhausted every alternative. For example, Bruno Latour pointed out in his 1988 book, *The Pasteurization of France*, that Pasteur received criticism for hasty generalizations made from too few cases.

Five years after Latour, historian Gerald Geison made the same complaint. From his reading of Pasteur's laboratory notebooks, he concluded that in 1885, Pasteur treated two young boys, both having been bitten by rabid dogs, with an untested vaccine. Geison noted that the ethical standards violated by Pasteur were his own.

Geison also claimed, again from his reading of the notebooks, that the vaccine used at Pouilly le Fort was prepared according to the method of a veterinarian from Toulouse who was not credited.

Other recent critics include scientists Charles and Jacqueline Reynolds. In their 1992 book, they conceded that Pasteur was the flag bearer for the germ theory of fermentation and disease. They noted, however, that he did not do studious research that defined microorganisms and studied their life cycles. They also complained that he did not originate the germ theory.

Charles Nicolle, Nobel Laureate and colleague of Roux, showed in the following anecdote a petty side of Pasteur.

The day before the Pouilly le Fort experiment was complete, Pasteur was at first erroneously informed that some of the inoculated sheep were sick. He was certain that the experiment was properly designed, and he refused to consider the possibility that it was not. Roux, who had conducted the vaccinations, came in for unfair and severe criticism. Mme. Pasteur's attempts to calm her husband had no effect. Furious, Pasteur declared he would not go to the scene to be shamed; Roux, because he was responsible, would go and endure the disgrace. But when Pasteur arrived at the station the next day, knowing by then that the sheep in the field were in the conditions he predicted, no hint of his recent concern was detected. His showmanship was evident when he cried out in triumph, "Well, men of little faith!"

Less than admirable was Pasteur's attitude toward Germany. There is no doubt of his sincere love for France; he served his country selflessly throughout his life and unceasingly urged that she maintain leadership in science. Here are some excerpts from his reflections on the fact that that leadership had been lost.

> Our disasters of 1870 [the Franco-Prussian War] are present in the mind of everyone . . . . Oh, my country! You who so long held the scepter of thought, why did you neglect your noblest creations? They are the divine torch which illuminates the world, the live source of the highest sentiments, which keep us free from sacrificing everything to material satisfactions . . . .

In the light of such patriotic feeling, Pasteur's returning his honorary M.D. to the University of Bonn in 1871 was understandable. But a quarter of a century later, he refused to accept from the Berlin Academy of Sciences the Order of Merit.

Ungracious as it appears, that refusal may well have been in accord with his stated philosophy that, "If science has no country, the scientist should have one, and ascribe to it the influence which his works may have in this world."

Metchnikoff who knew Pasteur, gave him this tribute:

"Like every one of us, Pasteur had his weaknesses, but even without mentioning the innumerable benefits he heaped on humanity, it must be said that he combined with his genius a vibrant soul, a goodness of heart, and an extraordinary loftiness of character."

Even though Pasteur had deficiencies, it is important to concentrate on the positive aspects of the man as a model scientist. Today, research has become so specialized and dependent on the team approach as well as on technology that Pasteur's 19th-century, solo, bench-type approach would not be possible for any large project. But obviously he had assets, in addition to genius, that would benefit the modern investigator.

Resourcefulness tops the list. Pasteur attacked and solved a variety of problems, often in fields that initially were unfamiliar to him. He had some luck and some significant contributions from colleagues and assistants, but his success was too consistent to be due to chance. (Some authorities believe that Roux, in particular, made very valuable contributions.)

Perseverance is also a very important trait. "My only strength resides in my tenacity," Pasteur said. Assiduous work was his life: "I would consider it a bad deed to let one day go without working." For him, the laboratory had to be quiet, free of visitors and even comfortable furniture. He spoke of "the serene peace of laboratories and libraries." When he could no longer do experimental work by himself, he kept himself thoroughly acquainted with whatever his assistants were doing. There is no doubt that his work was a consuming part of Pasteur's life; money was less important. "Let us work," he said, "this is the only thing which is entertaining." He was devoted to his wife and children, but much of the time he must have seemed remote to them.

Pasteur maintained that if he had his life to live over again, he would always try to remember a saying of Bossuet*: "The greatest

---

*Jacques Benigne Bossuet (1627-1704) was a bishop and a most eloquent and influential spokesman for the rights of the French church against papal authority.

---

aberration of the mind consists in believing a thing because it is desirable." The inference is that he valued a realistic approach to the experimental method.

Careful recording had a high priority in Pasteur' mind; indeed, the recording of his experiments received the same attention as the experiments themselves. Never content with an equivocal or dubious result, Pasteur repeated a given experiment until he was satisfied with it. Once assured that it was reproducible, he regarded the result as irrefutable.

"Enthusiasm is the god within, who leads to everything," Pasteur declared. And again: "The grandeur of human actions is measured by the inspiration from which they spring." There seems to have been an element of the dramatic about some of his demonstrations. And this approach was effective; the enthusiasm that radiated from Pasteur was a major factor in his success in changing the attitude of doubters.

Observation was one of Pasteur's strongest points. Combined with his theoretical knowledge and intuition, it served him well. According to historian Roderick McGrew, Pasteur made the first clear observation of bacterial antagonism; in 1877, he and Joubert described how rapidly anthrax bacilli multiplied when added to sterile urine, whereas addition of "common bacilli" halted the growth of anthrax. (Practical application of this type of phenomenon did not come until the advent of penicillin.)

Loir told of his uncle's extraordinary ability to notice what escaped other individuals. Pasteur, Loir himself, and others each looked at slices of bread cut from the same loaf. Pasteur found small fragments of wool, also roach and flour worm parts; the others found nothing unusual in their bread. And this was not an isolated case. It was customary for Pasteur, at almost every meal, to lay on the table such extraneous samples. To Loir, this was an outstanding memory of the great scientist.

Judgment was not lacking in Pasteur. About that, Duclaux wrote, "His rule was to attack at once the most important things and to neglect the trifles." This ability was intertwined with his experience and intuition.

Godfrey Hardy, one of the twentieth century's finest mathematical thinkers, listed ambition as a highly respectable motive, important in research. He included desire for reputation, position — even the power or the money which it brings. Pasteur certainly qualified there.

All these characteristics gave Pasteur confidence, a quality necessary in his struggle to change the thinking of a generation not attracted to the new germ theory.

Here is Duclaux's summary of Pasteur as a scientist:

> At the same time audacious and prudent, deceiving himself even for a long period but being brought back constantly to the true path by that exacting experimental method of which he has so often spoken gratefully, he is always worthy of admiration and worthy also to serve as an example.

The enduring significance of scientific discovery is often difficult to assess until after a lapse of time. The following represent opinions on Pasteur expressed by individuals versed in science or the history of science – individuals who were not his contemporaries.

In this century, Nobel Laureate André Lwoff observed that Pasteur "forced into biology and medicine the germ of what is called, by political theoreticians, permanent revolution."

George Rosen, an authority on public health, pointed out that although Pasteur often worked on pressing technical problems, he was concerned with broader ramifications. For example, his studies of fermentation led him to consider that minute living things might also be involved in producing putrid and suppurative diseases.

In John Hart's 1978 book entitled *The 100: A Ranking of the Most Influential Persons in History*, Pasteur is number 12. In Hart's own words:

> Since the mid-nineteenth century, life expectancies in much of the world have roughly doubled . . . . Pasteur's contributions are so fundamental that there is no question that he deserves the largest share of the credit for the decline in death rates that has occurred in the last century . . .

While it is true that some progress toward the control of diseases was made before specific microorganisms were implicated, most of the preventive measures tried were useless. An example of this is the 19th-century practice of burning bituminous coal in the belief that the smoke would prevent cholera. Today there is no clue to the etiology of human brain tumors; consequently we have no reasonable idea of how to prevent them. Such was the pre-Pasteur situation for many of the bacterial diseases.

In 1900, 18 percent of the population of the United States was in the age group older than 45 years. The average life span was 47 years. By 1950, 30 per cent of the population belonged to this group, and the life span had increased to 68 years. Today there is an analogous situation in some parts of the developing world as sanitation and vaccination are adopted. In fact, when infant deaths are cut, the ensuing population increase may be great enough and the effects disastrous enough to spur serious consideration of contraceptive measures.

The fact that in the United States the current figure for life expectancy is around 76 years is certainly not due to Pasteur alone. Sulfa drugs, introduced in the 1930's, and antibiotics, available since the 1940's, had a marked influence. Nutrition, education, housing, and other social factors played a role; advancements in dentistry must have made a considerable difference; the natural history of diseases may have changed, or the virulence of some microorganisms. Nonetheless, knowing the causative organism is an important step in the ultimate control of a disease.

With routine childhood immunizations, diseases such as diphtheria and poliomyelitis have just about disappeared in the developed world. On the whole, these countries have fought infectious diseases so well that they are now faced with a growing population of individuals prone to circulatory disease, cancer, neurological diseases, and other nonmicrobial conditions.

It soon became clear that Pasteur, in the end, had been so successful in imparting his ideas that there was an initial overemphasis on the germ theory of disease. As success followed success in the field of bacteriology, some investigators tended to believe that certain noninfectious disorders were caused by microorganisms yet to be discovered. Beriberi and pellagra, for example, are serious disorders due to vitamin deficiency. But that was not known in the early 20th century, and for a short time, much futile effort was expended in searching for their causative organisms.

A similar situation existed with cancer. Researchers erroneously claimed that various bacteria, fungi, and such were responsible for malignancies. However, by 1910, scientists were of the opinion that they were on the wrong track to search for a microorganism as the cause of human cancer. (In 1978, Robert Gallo reported the first human malignancy to be caused by a microorganism – in this case, a virus. Authorities currently believe that there are many types of carcinogens, including certain viruses.)

In line with Hart, Isaac Asimov, author and scientist, gave this appraisal of Pasteur: "In biology it is doubtful that anyone but Aristotle and Darwin can be mentioned in the same breath with him."

Figure 6-1 – Edelfeld's protrait of Pasteur. Today it hangs in the Louvre. *(Courtesy National Library of Medicine)*

Chapter 7

THE PASTEUR INSTITUTE, 1887-1900

Although its first focus had been on rabies, the Pasteur Institute was destined to become prominent in many fields of medical and scientific endeavor. Of special note were the accomplishments of early researchers which occurred during the period that ended with the beginning of a new century.

One of the diseases under early investigation was diphtheria, at the time an important child killer. Edwin Klebs and Friedrich Loeffler, two Germans, had pinned down a specific bacillus, *Corynebacterium diphtheriae*, as the causative organism, and Loeffler had suggested that a poison emitted by the microbe was responsible for the symptoms.

At the Institute, Roux and a colleague named Alexandre Yersin studied the mechanism of the bacterium's virulence. They found that a potent toxin produced in the throat by the organism was absorbed and carried by the blood to all parts of the body. This accounted for the damage to the heart and nervous system so often encountered in the disease. Roux then correctly defined diphtheria as an intoxication caused by a very active toxin formed by the bacillus within a localized area where it reproduced itself. This concept is fundamental to understanding the treatment of diphtheria and would be extended to some other diseases.

The next logical step was to find a way to neutralize the dangerous toxin. Roux and Yersin injected horses with increasingly stronger doses of bacterial toxin and succeeded in producing antitoxin. The immune horse serum that resulted could then be given to a person suffering from the disease. As we have noted, this procedure is called passive immunization. It is a therapeutic, rather than a preventive, measure. Because there is no stimulus (antigen), no additional antibody is produced, and the effectiveness of the antiserum rapidly diminishes.

Preceding Roux, Karl Fraenkel in Germany had shown that the injection of attenuated diphtheria bacilli would produce an immune guinea pig serum. In 1890, Emil von Behring, who, with Shibasaburo Kitasato of Japan, had made basic investigations on tetanus antitoxin, reported that a specific immune blood serum could be used to treat diphtheria as well. On Christmas night, 1891, a child in Berlin became the first human to be treated with diphtheria antitoxin.

Although von Behring is credited with the discovery of diphtheria antitoxin, serotherapy was not in general use until after Roux, in 1894, reported his results to an international congress in Budapest. With his co-workers, Roux had systematically treated children at one Paris hospital with the antidiphtheric serum, and used untreated children at another hospital as controls. In a four-month period, the mortality rate at the hospital where the control children with diphtheria were cared for was 60 percent. In the same period, at the hospital where the new treatment was in use, the mortality was 24 percent. We should note that science historians consider the medically trained Pierre Paul Emilie Roux one of Pasteur's most able and valuable collaborators.

With diphtheria being such a serious threat, there was soon a demand that the immune serum be made available to medical practitioners and that they be trained in its use. The *Figaro* newspaper opened an endowment to aid children with diphtheria and soon collected more than a million francs for the Institute. It was then able to buy horses and stables needed for permanent production of antiserum. In a three-month period, 50,000 doses were given away.

Pasteur, his death imminent, had been aware and proud of the progress being made. In fact, he spent his last days at the Institute's Park of Villeneuve-l'Etang, where his family had been provided living accommodations. The structure also stabled old military and race horses which were now destined to produce diphtheria antitoxin, but apparently Pasteur enjoyed being there. Perhaps it brought back memories of his rabies research carried out at Villeneuve-l'Etang.

Although antitoxin was very useful in treating acute cases of diphtheria, it could cause serious allergic reactions. Classic diphtheria is rarely seen today in the developed world, thanks to vigorous immunization programs. When it does occur, antibiotic treatment is used. During World War II, a cutaneous form of diphtheria caused serious trouble for military personnel stationed in Burma. Currently, this type of skin diphtheria is seen occasionally in the United States.

Duclaux, Pasteur's mainstay for many years, was instrumental in starting the Institute's own monthly journal, known as *Les annales de l'Institut Pasteur.* Just before he died, Pasteur was proud to read in the journal of another feat by Yersin. (Today, reports of scientific investigations at the Pasteur Institute appear in a wide variety of publications read by researchers from all over the globe.)

Yersin, now working in the French colonies, had gone to Hong Kong in 1894 to study an epidemic of bubonic plague. He found the causative organism, today named *Yersinia pestis.* (Kitasato made the same discovery independently.) Tragically, Jews had sometimes been massacred when the terrible bubonic plague struck during the 14th century. Through ignorance, they, rather than the microbe, had been blamed for the disaster.

In 1897, a countryman of Kitasato named Ogatia suggested that fleas from infected rats might transmit the disease to man. The next year, Paul Louis Simond, a Pastorian (an investigator at the Pasteur Institute), showed that plague was primarily a disease of rats, not man, and was spread by rat fleas. Plague should not be considered a dreaded affliction only of the past; it is still a dangerous menace in parts of both the eastern and southern hemispheres. Of course, knowledge of its cause and transmission aids immeasurably in providing adequate control of the disease.

Pasteur naturally encouraged non-French scientists to study in his laboratory. One of the most famous of these was Elie Metchnikoff, a Russian.

After some years as a professor of zoology and comparative anatomy in Odessa, Metchnikoff resigned to devote himself to research. In Messina, Italy, he made microscopic studies of starfish larvae. One experiment was crucial; he placed a few rose thorns under the skin of some of the larvae — skin that he described as transparent as water. His theory was that the thorns, being "foreign bodies" would soon become engulfed by wandering scavenger cells.

Metchnikoff recounted that he was too excited to sleep that night. Very early the next morning he had the satisfaction of seeing that his assumption was correct. "That experiment formed the basis of the phagocyte theory, to the development of which I devoted the next twenty-five years of my life," he wrote.

His finding, familiar today as the first line of defense in the body's immunologic response, was not readily accepted in scientific circles. As Metchnikoff sought a congenial atmosphere where he could pursue the problem, he considered the laboratories of both Pasteur and Koch. The latter was for some years unreceptive to the idea of phagocytosis. But not Pasteur.

Metchnikoff accepted an invitation to come to Paris in 1880, and he remained at the Institute until his death in 1916. Metchnikoff described his first interview with Pasteur:

"On arriving at the laboratory destined for the antirabic vaccinations, I saw an old man, rather undersized, with a left hemiplegia, very piercing grey eyes, a short beard and moustache and slightly grey hair, covered by a black skullcap. The pale and sickly complexion and tired look betokened a man who was not likely to live many more years."

Pasteur received the newcomer with kindness. He assured the younger man that he agreed with his ideas about the defenses of the body, and expressed the belief that he was on the right road.

Metchnikoff was indeed on the right road, and his reward would come; with Paul Ehrlich, the father of chemotherapy, he shared the 1908 Nobel Prize for Physiology and Medicine.

The Russian was so satisfied with the atmosphere of the Institute that, in 1889, he had asked a countryman, Waldemar Haffkine, to join him to work on an anticholera vaccine. In 1893, Haffkine was ready to go to India, then the source of a great cholera epidemic. He worked under extreme difficulties, but was able to show that inoculated persons had about one tenth the morbidity and mortality of the uninoculated.

Today, such prophylactic vaccination is little used; cholera epidemics are prevented by the practice of good public health measures. Knowledge about fluid and electrolyte balance in the body has led to improved treatment of cholera and other diarrheal diseases, but cholera still presents a serious public health challenge.

Later, Haffkine worked on immunization against plague. His vaccine often produced undesirable effects, but it reduced mortality by 20 to 30 percent. Modern preventive measures for this disease are, for the most part, rodent control and the avoidance of flea bites, but an oral vaccine is available.

Another Russian protege of Pasteur was Nikola Fedorvich Gamalia, who, in Odessa, founded the first laboratory outside France for the treatment of rabies. There would be many other such satellite Pasteur Institutes to come.

The success of a vaccine depends on the response of the body. Some basic facts about the process were discovered many years ago; some are relatively new; few of them were known in Pasteur's day; much is not clear even today.

When a foreign substance invades the body, it encounters a line of defense that is nonspecific in nature. Part of this defense is the unbroken skin, the protective secretions of the mucous membranes, and the acidity of the gastric juice. An important part of the defense process is phagocytosis, or being eaten by a cell. Certain wandering cells of the blood, known as neutrophils and monocytes[*], can engulf bacteria (and other foreign particulates – the response is nonspecific) and may draw them into the cell's interior where they are killed and liquefied by enzymatic action. Killer cells may destroy tumor cells and virus-infected cells. Fixed cells outside the blood vessels may also participate in the action.

Pus is the result of phagocytic activity; it contains huge numbers of white blood cells that have accumulated locally to combat bacterial invasion. Participating also in defense is the complement system, consisting of a number of circulating proteins, which facilitate not only phagocytosis but other processes such as vascular permeability and cell lysis.

---

[*]Some authors use the terms monocyte and macrophage as synonyms. Most use the term monocyte to refer to the phagocytic cells in the peripheral blood and macrophage to those fixed in the tissues.

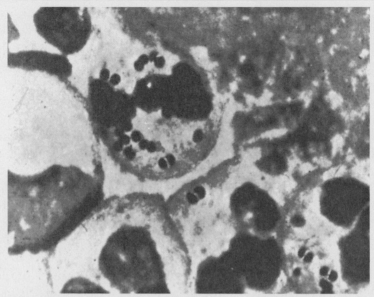

Figure 7-1 – Pus cells with engulfed meningococci from cerebrospinal fluid, magnified 1,500 times. From J. Shaffer and M. Goldin, *Todd-Sanford Clinical Diagnosis by Laboratory Methods*, 14th ed., p. 842. *(Courtesy E. B. Saunders)*

Often such defense is sufficient to halt invasion. This is the case when a pimple forms and then disappears in the course of a few days. In this case, the invader is likely to be a staphylococcus. But, suppose the invader is the meningococcus, present in droplets coughed out by a carrier of cerebrospinal meningitis. After localizing in the victim's nasopharynx, the organism* enters the victim's bloodstream, producing septicemia. The infection is no longer local, and humoral antibodies are produced to overcome the infection.

A specific immune response is evoked by what is usually known as an antigen; some authorities prefer immunogen. An antigen is usually protein and often a microorganism or a product of a microorganism. It has been estimated that there are one million different antigens to which the human immune system can react directly.

The lymphocytes involved in defense mechanisms are indistinguishable under the light microscope. Those that originate in the bone marrow but are not exposed to the thymus gland are called B cells. Constituting 10 to 20 percent of the lymphocyte population,

*The bacterium is of course reproducing itself. In all probability, many meningococci, not just one, would be present in the droplets.

these B cells differentiate into plasma cells that produce antibodies responsible for the so-called humoral response mounted usually against bacteria.

Lymphocytes that migrate to the thymus gland during development are named T cells. They play a role in delayed hypersensitivity, organ transplantation rejection, and resistance to viruses, fungi, some bacteria, and possibly tumors. T cells are crucial to what is known as the cell-mediated response and are longer-lived than B cells, remaining in existence for a decade or so. Killer T cells attack and destroy foreign cells. Helper T cells aid B lymphocytes (as well as other T cells) in making an optimum immunological response, although they do not produce humoral antibodies. Suppressor T cells can cut off the response when it is sufficient.

Antibodies are proteins that are part of the blood plasma and are known as immunoglobulins. The surface of the B cell contains specific receptors that are molecules of immunoglobulins. When antigen enters the body, it reacts with the lymphocyte that makes the best fit with the surface receptor. The binding that takes place causes the B cell to proliferate, producing a clone of immunocompetent cells that produce the specific antibody. A given B cell can respond to only one kind of antigen or group of closely related antigens.

The 1970's saw a major advance in the laboratory production of antibodies. This process produces large quantities of antibody in a reproducible manner. These monoclonal antibodies, in contrast to those raised in animals, contain no nonspecific antibodies. They are also most useful in diagnostic testing.

Vaccines confer *active* immunity. This means that over a short time period the antigen in question produces antibodies that are effective in preventing a disease or its serious effects when the same antigen challenges the body at a later date.

Today, an infant routinely receives shots to prevent diphtheria, tetanus, and pertussis (DTP). He is given *Hemophilus influenzae*, type B (HIB) vaccine and an oral, live attenuated three-strain vaccine for poliomyelitis (OPV.) He is also immunized against measles, mumps, and rubella. A vaccine for hepatitis B virus (HBV) is injected into the deltoid muscle.

The antigens for diphtheria and tetanus are not bacterial bodies, but rather the chemically treated toxins that they produce. Likewise, the antigen for *Hemophilas B* is a complex carbohydrate substance extracted from the capsule of the organism; HBV consists of the viral surface antigen. Unless the child's immune system is defective, he will build up antibodies against the pertussis and the *Hemophilus B* bacilli and against the deleterious toxins produced by diphtheria and tetanus bacilli. A *booster* shot is effective because it rapidly marshals a reservoir of B-cell derivatives that are still antigen-sensitive from a previous exposure.

Passive immunity refers to the practice of injecting donated antibodies. These are antibodies raised in another person or animal either during the natural course of the disease or by vaccination, or they are antibodies produced *in vitro* by modern methods. Donated antibodies become ineffective in a few weeks, but will afford immediate protection for a short period. As an example, if an individual whose immunity to tetanus has waned and who is thought to be at risk, passive immunization could be conferred by the administration of tetanus immune globulin. The rabies immune globulin mentioned earlier would also confer passive immunity against that disease.

Vaccines are not without risk; serious allergic reactions may develop, and there is always the possibility that a live vaccine may revert to its original form and so become the cause, rather than the prevention, of the disease. The risk of such a mishap, however, is outweighed by the risk presented when no protection is provided. Fortunately, biotechnology, coupled with better understanding of the immune system, is making possible so-called subunit vaccines containing necessary antigenic units but devoid of potentially dangerous components.

Immunization programs are most effective in the young, but offer benefits for adults, also. For instance, adults should receive tetanus shots every ten years throughout life, and oldsters should have annual flu shots. A polysaccharide vaccine can protect geriatric patients from pneumococcal pneumonia.

Pasteur's legacy is reflected in the list of available preventive vaccines against human diseases that may occur throughout the world. The diseases include cerebrospinal meningitis, cholera, diphtheria, German measles (rubella), haemophilus influenza infection, hepatitis B, influenza, measles (rubeola), mumps, paratyphoid, plague, pneumococcic pneumonia, poliomyelitis, rabies, tetanus, tuberculosis, typhoid, typhus, yellow fever, and whooping cough (pertussis). Vaccines against various animal diseases play an important role in world economics.

Following Metchnikoff, the next Pasteur scientist to win the most coveted of all scientific prizes was a Belgian, Jules Jean-Baptiste Vincent Bordet. Working at the Institute during the years 1894 to 1901, Bordet discovered the important mechanism known as complement fixation, whereby red blood cells and bacteria are destroyed. This enabled the later development of various diagnostic procedures, in particular, one of the early laboratory tests for syphilis known as the Wassermann. Bordet, in collaboration with a colleague named Octave Gengou, discovered the whooping cough bacillus in 1906. He also founded and directed a Pasteur Institute in Brabant, Belgium. He was awarded the Nobel Prize for Medicine and Physiology in 1919.

The last five years of the nineteenth century brought momentous events in France and elsewhere. A victim of anti-Semitism, Captain Alfred Dreyfus was imprisoned on Devil's Island for a crime he did not commit; the Klondike gold rush took place at Bonanza Creek in Canada; Edmund Rostand wrote *Cyrano de Bergerac*; Queen Victoria's Diamond Jubilee was celebrated; the Spanish-American War began in 1898 and the Boer War the following year.

There were extraordinary events in science and technology, also. Wilhelm Konrad Röntgen discovered x-rays, and almost immediately there were medical applications for his finding. Antoine Henri Becquerel discovered radioactivity in uranium, spurring future research by Pierre and Marie Curie. The electron was discovered and cathode rays were investigated. The first photographs utilizing artificial light were produced. The first magnetic recording of sound was reported and human speech was transmitted via radio waves. By 1900, Sigmund Freud's *Dreams* was causing amazement to both medical and lay readers, while Toulouse-Lautrec, Picasso, and Gouguin were becoming well known to the world of art.

Chapter 8

THE PASTEUR INSTITUTE, 1901-1918

Early in the 20th century, additional buildings were added to the Pasteur Institute — biochemistry laboratories, a hospital for the treatment of infectious diseases, and a consultation building. In collaboration with the University of Paris, a Radium Institute was created for application of Marie Curie's discoveries.

Pasteur did not live to see the establishment of the Laboratory of Tropical Diseases at his Institute. The founder was Charles Louis Alphonse Laveran, a French parasitologist and military physician. In 1880, while studying malarial fever in Algeria, he had discovered the parasite responsible* for the disease (*Plasmodium falciparum*) in human red blood cells. Associated with the Pasteur Institute from 1897 to 1922, he was awarded a 1907 Nobel Prize for his research on protozoan disease agents.

Malaria exemplifies a very important protozoan disease. It was known in antiquity and has a worldwide existence. Its effects have been devastating. Although populations such as the people of West Africa had developed some immunity to the virulent *Plasmodium falciparum*, malaria was very destructive when previously unexposed people migrated to regions where malaria was endemic.

---

*The word *malaria* was coined by an Italian in 1753. He believed that bad air was responsible for the disease because it frequently affected persons living near swamps or bodies of stagnant, smelly water.

Most Americans today associate malaria with Asia and Africa, little realizing how prevalent the disease had once been in the continental United States. Its decline was related to the rise of modern agriculture, but in the rural South there were as many as one million cases a year as late as 1915. The drainage of swamps and other breeding places of the mosquito is an important part of malaria control. With the availability of dichloro-diphenyl-trichloro-ethane (DDT) and other insecticides after World War II, malaria virtually disappeared from the United States. In some countries, however, the problem is still far from solved.

A Pasteur Institute scientist who gained recognition during the first decade of the 1900's was Amedée Borrel, for whom the genus Borrelia (of spirochetes) is named. At the Institute, he worked to develop a vaccine for plague and is best remembered for a 1907 publication in the Bulletin of the Institute. In this, he presented his beliefs that some cancers had a viral etiology. Four years later, his theory was confirmed by experiment. Peyton Rous of the United States published evidence that sarcomas in chickens could be induced by an agent that passed through a bacterial filter. For this, Rous belatedly received a Nobel Prize in 1966.

Another who brought fame to the Pasteur Institute around this same time was Constantin Levaditi, a Romanian bacteriologist. In collaboration with Karl Landsteiner of Vienna, he showed that poliomyelitis was caused by a virus. The Levaditi silver impregnation method, used to demonstrate *Treponema pallidum* in sections of tissue, was named for him. *Treponema pallidum* is the spirochete that causes syphilis.

In 1909, Charles Jean Nicolle discovered that classical, or epidemic, typhus fever was transmitted by the body louse, *Pediculus corpori*. This work brought Nicolle the Nobel Prize in 1923. He had worked at the Pasteur Institute with Roux. Later he served from 1922-32 as director of the Pasteur Institute, Tunis. In contrast to the situation with malaria, the vector for typhus was discovered before the causative organism.

Epidemic typhus has been one of mankind's greatest killers, especially in the aftermath of war. It was first recognized in 1083 at a monastery near Salerno. Spanish explorers brought it to the Americas, where it caused terrible havoc among Indian populations. Even during this century – between 1918 and 1922 – typhus claimed the lives of some three million Russians.

The causative agent was identified in 1914 by Stanislas J. M. von Prowazek, who died of typhus in the course of his investigations. In 1916, Henrique de Rocha-Lima of Brazil extended von Prowazek's work. An American, Howard T. Ricketts, had first identified the genus (now *Rickettsia*) to which Rocky Mountain spotted fever and epidemic typhus belong. He, too, died of the disease he was studying. The pathogen responsible for typhus is named *Rickettsia prowazekii*.

When an infected body louse bites, it defecates at the same time. The organisms present in the feces soon penetrate the skin. Louse infestation results from overcrowding and poor hygiene, conditions associated with war and famine. In 1935, Hans Zinsser, who was a distinguished investigator at Harvard Medical School, wrote a popular, but authoritative, book about classical typhus – *Rats, Lice and History.*

Paul Ehrlich of Frankfort, Germany, is considered the father of chemotherapy. In 1904, he developed Salvarsan, an arsenic-based compound that was effective against *Treponema pallidum*, the organism that causes syphilis. Salvarsan was also known as 606 because it represented the number of experiments needed to produce and select it.

In the same year, the Pasteur Institute was trying anti-infection chemotherapy. Seven years later, a Chemotherapy Center was created and antibacterial and antiparasitic compounds were developed.

In 1915, while World War I was in progress, a Canadian named Felix d'Herelle, who was working at the Pasteur Institute, discovered bacteriophage. He was investigating a dysentery epidemic that had struck a cavalry squadron quartered near Paris. The cause was the Shiga bacillus rather than the protozoan parasite, *Entamoeba histolytica**. When he grew the bacillus on agar plates, he sometimes noticed clear, round areas where there was no bacterial growth. These he named *taches vierges* (untouched spots). They are now known as plaques.

D'Herelle concentrated on the feces of one sick man, taking daily samples for four days to determine any correlation between changes in the man's clinical condition and changes in the plaques. A

---

*The disorder it caused was bacillary dysentery, not amebic dysentery.

suspension of feces was passed through a Chamberland filter – one designed to hold back bacteria. The bacteria-free filtrate was then added to a broth culture of Shiga bacilli, and an agar plate was inoculated with the mixture. The next day, the plate showed no growth. Also, broth cultures that had been turbid – an indication of bacterial growth – had cleared over night.

D'Herelle concluded that the plaques were due to a filterable agent, parasitic on the bacteria. Such an agent we now call a bacteriophage, or phage, and recognize it as a virus whose host is a bacterium. In 1892, a Russian botanist named Dmetri Iwanowski found that the agent causing mosaic disease in tobacco could not be held back by a porcelain filter made to retain ordinary bacteria. Two years later, this fact was confirmed by Martinus Beijerinck, a Dutch botanist. Beijerinck stated firmly that the infectious agent was not bacterial in nature.

At this time in history, there was no knowledge of how to grow viruses; also they could not be seen with the ordinary light microscope. Viruses were identified by their action, as Pasteur had identified the rabies virus, and as d'Herelle had done.

D'Herelle surmised that at the time when the virus *in vitro* had vanquished the bacillus, the *in vivo* action would be similar. In other words, the patient would be much improved. A visit to the hospital showed d'Herelle that this was the case.

Over the next three years, d'Herelle found 34 cases of dysentery that seemed to fit his hypothesis. In addition, bacteriophages were isolated from other diseases – cholera, anthrax, diphtheria. Bacteriophage therapy became an attractive idea, which D'Herelle promoted. Unfortunately, it was not successful. Despite research done for more than 20 years in various parts of the world, bacteriophage therapy did not fulfil its promise of curing bacterial disease.

Some of d'Herelle's efforts were more productive. He developed what is called the plaque assay, a method for counting viruses. He demonstrated that it was necessary for a phage to attach to a bacterium to do damage, and that there is a specificity involved. D'Herelle also showed that phage replication is cyclic. Later, these bacterial viruses became valuable models for the study of fundamental biological processes at the molecular level.

Ironically, the bacteriophage had also been discovered in Britain, and the finding was published two years before d'Herelle's. The

British discovery was made in 1915 by Frederick W. Twort. Twort was trying to grow vaccinia virus on artificial media. This he failed to do. However, his agar became contaminated with bacterial colonies. In time, there appeared to develop transparent areas, undergoing what he termed "glassy transformation." He found that an infinitesimal amount of the glassy material would kill bacteria; the material could pass through a bacterial filter and remain active; heat would destroy the agent.

Twort published a brief account in the Lancet, a medical journal, noting that a virus capable of killing bacteria had been identified. Military service followed for him and, when peace came, he pursued other interests. D'Herelle's discovery was completely independent of Twort's. Apparently, d'Herelle had not read the material in the Lancet. Considering that Europe was embroiled in a ghastly war, this is not unusual.

Metchnikoff's account of conditions at the Institute during World War I gives us a glimpse of the grim situation in Paris. Research had stopped because of a lack of animals. The Institute's stables were filled with cows to provide milk for hospitals and children's homes. Only females and old men remained, since laboratory attendants, as well as young investigators and their assistants, were all in the military.

Gounod's Faust was presented at the 1918 opening of the Paris Opera. That year saw momentous events: the Germans bombed Paris; Czar Nicholas of Russia (then technically ex-czar) and his family were executed; Kaiser Wilhelm II of Germany abdicated. After the war ended in November of 1918, the casualties had amounted to approximately 8.5 million killed, 21 million wounded, and 7.5 million taken prisoner or considered missing. These figures would get worse, for a great pandemic of influenza had begun.

In the United States, the first Chicago-New York airmail had been delivered — flying time 10 hours, 5 minutes; daylight saving time had been introduced; the Mount Wilson telescope in California was completed; and the country's total population now stood at 103.5 million.

Chapter 9

THE PASTEUR INSTITUTE, 1919-1945

The period from 1919 to 1945 was not the brightest in the Institute's history. As a privately funded organization, it suffered during the depression years of the 1930's. Expansion was curtailed, and there was little money to buy new equipment. With World War II came the German occupation of Paris with its attendant evil. Even so, at the same time, there was significant progress in science.

One advance involved the control of tuberculosis. Tuberculosis was known to the ancient world. Hippocratic writings from before Christ described it, but the condition was not considered contagious. On the other hand, Galen (A.D. 130-200) did recognize its infectious nature. In 1865, a French pathologist named Jean Antoine Villemine demonstrated that material from a person dying of tuberculosis could cause the disease in animals. Autopsy records from early in the nineteenth century show that, at the L'Hopital de la Charité in Paris, tuberculosis was the cause of death in roughly 30 percent of the cases. During the same century, the disease was so familiar that fictional characters, even in opera, were sometimes afflicted. As noted previously, Robert Koch's identification of the causative organism in 1882 was a critical event.

The overwhelming majority of the cases seen were classified as the pulmonary type due to *Mycobacterium tuberculosis*. Its presence in the sputum meant that coughing by the patient was likely to spread the disease; uninfected individuals were at risk when they inhaled these droplets.

A minority of the cases were caused by *Mycobacterium bovis,* which is not spread by airborne droplets. This organism may be present in infected milk which has not been pasteurized. When an individual – often a child – drank milk contaminated with the bovine strain, he was likely to contract a form of the disease that involved the lymph glands or the skeletal system rather than the more familiar form that affected the lungs.

There were differences in severity, but, in general, the outlook was grim. It was soon recognized that tuberculosis was associated with social conditions such as crowding and poor nutrition. The incidence of the disease rose under the stress of war; for instance, deaths from tuberculosis increased in 1870 and 1871, one of the periods when Paris was under siege.

With no cure at hand, various scientists sought to produce a preventive vaccine. Success was attained by Albert Calmette and Camille Guérin at the Pasteur Institute in Lille. By culturing over a long period of time, they obtained a strain of *Mycobacterium bovis* that they believed was stable with regard to virulence. By 1928, 116,000 infants in France had received BCG vaccine (for *Bacillus Calmette-Guérin*); it was also used in other countries.

In 1930, disaster struck; in Lübeck, Germany, 72 of 251 vaccinated persons succumbed to tuberculosis contracted from the vaccine. Although it is generally conceded that a bottle of the vaccine was contaminated with virulent organisms, the tragedy prolonged resistance to the use of the vaccine. Eventually, sufficient statistical evidence accumulated to show that BCG vaccination produces increased resistance to tuberculosis for a limited period.

During the years 1932-38, the Institute's André Michael Lwoff provided important information to science. With his wife, Marguerite, he showed that a vitamin may function not only as a bacterial growth factor, but also as part of a coenzyme, a compound necessary in certain cellular reactions. His *L'evolution physiologique* was published in 1941 and presented a theory of bacterial evolution.

The Pasteur Institute was associated with sulfanilamide, one of the first "wonder drugs." The story begins in Germany. While employed by the I. G. Farben drug subsidiary of the Bayer Corporation in Elberfeld, Gerhard Domagk made a systematic investigation of the antibacterial action of various chemicals. In the early 1930's, he found that a dye named Prontosil, when administered to mice, could overcome the lethal effect produced by a hemolytic streptococcus; the dye was also effective in humans. (A hemolytic streptococcus was the common cause of often fatal "blood poisoning.") Prontosil was patented by I. G. Farben in 1932.

Prontosil did not inhibit the growth of *in vitro* cultures of the same organism, presenting a puzzle to investigators. At the Pasteur Institute in 1936, Jacques and Thérèse Trefouel, husband and wife, with two other investigators, succeeded in showing that in the body, the active principle of Prontosil was released from the dye molecule. They identified it as sulfanilamide. (For a dramatic portrait of the importance of sulfa drugs, see Appendix 1.)

The Bayer Company had made a considerable investment in the development of Prontosil and had hoped to recover this investment and make a profit. Sulfanilamide, unlike Prontosil, could not be patented because of previous publications. With no patent, commercial production became competitive. In addition, the discovery opened the way for a search for chemicals similar in action to sulfanilamide. Thus, sulfa drugs saved countless lives before the advent of the antibiotic age in the 1940's.

Domagk was chosen to receive a Nobel Prize for his work, but a Nazi decree forced him to decline it. After the war, he went to Stockholm to be honored. Jacques Trefouel served as director of the Pasteur Institute from 1941-65.

One of the researchers associated with the Trefouels was Daniel Bovet. He would be awarded a 1957 Nobel Prize "for his discoveries concerning the synthetic compounds which inhibit the action of certain substances in the body and especially their action on the vascular system and the muscles of the skeleton." Bovet was born in Switzerland and received the degree of Doctor of Science from the University of Geneva. His tenure at the Pasteur Institute spanned the years 1929 to 1947, many of them spent as head of the laboratory of therapeutic chemistry. During his scientific career, Bovet's numerous publications included the areas of microbiology, toxicology, and endocrinology.

In 1944, he discovered the first antihistamine, a drug that counteracts the effects of histamine. Histamine is formed in the body and plays a part in allergic reactions, dilating small blood vessels and producing local reddening as well as a wheal, which is a swelling due to excess fluid formation; it also causes smooth muscle to contract. Allergic reactions vary in seriousness: they can cause minor discomfort or become life-threatening. Antihistamines are obviously aids to the practicing physician, and after the ground-breaking work of Bovet, others have been developed.

Bovet next concentrated on the medical use of skeletal relaxants. These are known as curarimimetics, and they interfere with the transmission of nerve impulses. The name is derived from curare, a substance obtained from certain tropical American plants. South American Indians used curare as an arrow poison, both in hunting and warfare. Its most important constituent is tubocurare. These muscle relaxants were auxiliaries in general anesthesia, especially in abdominal operations, and have been valuable in various medical situations where muscle relaxation is desirable.

On June 12, 1940, Paris was declared an open city. June 14 was a sad day for the City of Light – the Nazi occupation began. On that day, to avoid opening Pasteur's burial crypt for the Germans, the gatekeeper committed suicide. That gatekeeper was Joseph Meister, whom Pasteur had successfully treated for rabies.

Another tragic event occurred at the Institute during the occupation. Eugene and Elizabeth Wollman, who had been researchers at the Institute since 1919, had done outstanding work on bacteriophages. Their work, however, would never be completed; they were arrested in 1943 and deported to Auschwitz concentration camp in Poland.

After the Allies invaded continental Europe and were driving toward Berlin, Generals Eisenhower and Bradley thought it prudent to bypass Paris temporarily – that would have saved time and supplies. However, French partisans became so menacing to the occupying Germans that there was fear the Nazis would destroy the city. A plan was finally worked out by Raoul Nordling, the Swedish Consel General.

On August 25, 1944, General Jacques Le Clerc's Free French 2nd Armored Division, followed by the American 4th Infantry Division, accepted the surrender of the German commander, General Dietrich von Choltitz. Although he had been ordered by Hitler to demolish the city, Choltitz negotiated an agreement that left Paris intact. At long last, the leader of Free France, General Charles de Gaulle, marched down the Champs-Elysees amid tears, cheers, and cries of "Vive de Gaulle!"

V.E. Day, May 8, 1945, ended the war in Europe. On August 6, the United States Army Air Force dropped an atomic bomb on Hiroshima, Japan. A second such bomb demolished Nagasaki on August 9. Five days later, the Japanese surrendered. The number of war dead was estimated at 15 million, in addition to the 10 million who died in Nazi concentration camps.

Chapter 10

THE PASTEUR INSTITUTE, 1946 TO PRESENT

The period from the end of World War II until the present saw wondrous events.

Hiroshima raised the threat of nuclear destruction, and it was not long before the free world, led by the United States, was engaged in a cold war with the Soviet Union. The Korean War (1950-53) and the Vietnam War (1961-73) were related to this. The breakup of colonial empires spawned the emergence of Third World countries. The Space Age began in 1957 when the Soviets launched Sputniks I and II, the first earth-orbiting satellites. Four years later, Yuri Gagarin orbited the earth in a 6-ton Russian satellite. The Cold War ended in 1990 with the signing of the Charter of Paris for a new Europe. This decreed an end to "the era of confrontation and division . . . ."

Momentous changes in everyday life were wrought by transistors and semiconductors (computers, TV, video and audio systems); Xerox™ machines; jet propulsion; plastics and synthetic fibers; the contraceptive pill; antibiotics; cortisone; and a host of other products.

The discoveries in science were no less marvelous than the evolution of world events. Like the Golden Age of Bacteriology, this was a Golden Age of Molecular Biology. (For a more complete look at molecular biology, see Appendix 2.)

The Pasteur Institute had continued to grow ever since its founding. However, there had been financial difficulties — first the Depression and then a problem of a different sort. The success of antibiotics, to some extent, diminished the profits from vaccines and other biologicals — profits on which the Institute depended. Fortunately, the generosity of American foundations enabled the Pasteur Institute to compete in the postwar scientific world. In another vein, good rapport with American investigators was established as the United States became the leader of that world. Dedicated as it was to interdisciplinary research, the Pasteur Institute was, by the 1950's, focusing its resources on the many aspects of molecular biology.

André Lwoff, a Pastorian since 1921, became a leading light in virology. Lwoff was especially active in the classification and nomenclature of viruses. He and his colleagues coined such words as *virion*, *capsid*, and *capsomere*.

With the invention and development of the electron microscope, there was at last a means for visualizing viruses.

Viruses come in many sizes and shapes. An outer rigid structure, called the *capsid*, is made up of protein subunits (capsomeres) and encloses and protects a core of nucleic acid, the infectious material. A common arrangement of a virus particle, or virion, is in the form of an icosahedron, a three-dimensional structure with 30 edges, 12 corners, and 20 faces. The total number of capsomeres in the virion depends on the number packed into each face and is characteristic for each of these viruses. Other shapes are common; for example, rod-shaped (tobacco mosaic virus) or bullet shaped (rabies). Certain bacteriophages have remarkably complex structures — a polyhedral head, a tubular tail, jointed tail fibers, etc. Phages can attach to a bacterial cell and contract to force the infective nucleic acid into the host cell. Some viruses may have additional external coats such as membrane from its host cell. As noted previously, a virus is an obligate parasite and can be reproduced only within the cells of its host.

Lwoff's reputation was much enhanced by his postwar study of the phenomenon of lysogeny. The Wollmans, who perished in a concentration camp, had, in the Institute's *Annals*, published their reasoning that there must be both infectious and noninfectious phases in the life cycle of the Twort/d'Herelle phage. They had even purchased a micromanipulator to select single bacterial cells for experiment. Lwoff now continued their work. Using a bacillus as the host, he showed that viral DNA of the phage became part of the bacterial chromosome, replicating with the host cell without damage perhaps for several generations. Lwoff named this non-infective form *prophage*. He demonstrated that ultraviolet light, by damaging the bacterium and reducing its resistance to viral takeover, permitted the production of large numbers of new and complete infective viruses within the cell. These virus particles were released by lysing (dissolving) the bacterial cell. (The term lysogeny refers to this latter action.) These freed virions were now capable of invading new cells.

Lwoff apparently approached his work with the same infectious enthusiasm that characterized Pasteur. Perhaps this accounts for the quality of his associates. One of these was Jacques Lucien Monod, scientist and musician, who trained in zoology at the Sorbonne. Another was Francois Jacob, whose medical education was interrupted as he served with Free French forces and survived serious wounds. According to Jacob, in the attic laboratory where they worked with phage, "Lwoff and Monod had been able to produce an atmosphere in which mingled enthusiasm, intellectual clear-sightedness, non-conformity, and friendship."

Another protege of Lwoff was Elie Wollman, the son of the Wollmans and namesake of Elie Metchnikoff. He and Jacob combined their efforts to study bacterial conjugation, a type of sexual reproduction. (Bacteria multiply primarily by an asexual process of splitting into two halves.) Using the lambda phage, naturally carried as a prophage by certain strains of *Escherichia coli*, their genetic studies showed that the bacterial chromosome was a circular strand of DNA. The equipment required was not necessarily hi-tech: a blender essential to their experiments had originally been purchased in the United States to make purees for the Jacob children. The findings of Jacob and Wollman were published in book form in 1961 as *Sexuality and the Genetics of Bacteria*.

In 1958, Monod and Jacob combined their talents to form a very fruitful collaboration. They advanced the proposal that prophage was controlled by a repressor produced by a prophage gene. Free replication of phage in the cytosol was a result of inactivation of the repressor. To account for the control of protein synthesis during bacteriophage multiplication, the pair offered the hypothesis that the information for the synthesis of phage protein was carried to the ribosomes of the host cell by a new, unstable RNA in which the base sequence corresponded with that of phage DNA. This short-lived RNA is now familiar as mRNA (messenger RNA), and experiments that used molecular hybridization and other methods proved its existence.

On Christmas Eve, 1960, the pair mailed out for publication a paper that, in detail, presented their concepts of genetic regulatory mechanisms in the synthesis of protein. Their work would bring glory to the Pasteur Institute: five years later, Jacob, Lwoff, and Monod were awarded the Nobel Prize.

From 1971 to 1976, Monod served as the Institute's director. Lwoff noted, "It may seem strange that a devoted passionate scientist could, in full activity, abandon the laboratory. Perhaps he sensed that . . . he had reached the peak of his scientific achievements." Lwoff observed that the most likely hypothesis was that Monod's sense of duty played a determining role in his decision.

Jacques Oudin was a Pastorian who made his mark in immunology. He first claimed fame by devising a simple and useful test-tube method to identify an antigen by the precipitate formed when it combined with its specific antibody. His later more sophisticated discoveries of 1956 and 1965 involved spacial properties of two types of antibodies. Information of this nature could be valuable when new vaccines are under consideration.

By 1981, the disease named AIDS was known. By early 1983, scientists at the Pasteur Institute had identified the virus that is now considered the causative agent. They also showed that this virus did not belong to the human T-lymphotrophic virus (HTLV) group, as was first believed.

This identification came about because some French physicians believed that the virus at fault might be found early in the disease, before the destruction of T-helper cells. A Pasteur Institute group, headed by Luc Montagnier, was looking for evidence that retroviruses were involved in human cancers. Retroviruses are viruses which carry RNA rather than DNA, and are also equipped with an enzyme named reverse transcriptase. To replicate the virus, the enzyme produces a DNA copy (reverse transcription) from RNA. This DNA then codes for additional viral RNA and new virus.

Late in 1982, the doctors requested that Montagnier's team culture cells from a lymph node biopsy taken from a hospitalized homosexual patient afflicted with persistent swollen lymph nodes, one of the early symptoms of AIDS.

Two weeks passed before Françoise Barré-Sinoussi found evidence of reverse transcriptase activity in the culture, which pointed to the presence of a retrovirus. Electron microscopy soon corroborated this. Epidemiological data was obtained through collaboration with the Disease Control Center in Atlanta, which supplied test material isolated from similar cases. The complete nucleotide sequence was reported in early 1985.

An international committee ultimately decided on the name *human immunodeficiency virus* (HIV) to supplant the French lymphadenopathy-associated virus (LAV) and names used by other investigators. HIV is now classified as a member of the lentivirus group, which are retroviruses. Lenti (slow) viruses take years to manifest their consequences. In September, 1983, the Pasteur Institute filed a patent for an ELISA test that would identify antibodies to the virus in suspected patients, blood products, and blood donors.

Toward the end of 1985, Montagnier's team discovered another HIV virus, this time in inhabitants of West Africa. Again, an ELISA test for it was developed. By early 1987, the complete nucleotide sequence of that virus had been reported. The latter procedure showed

Figure 10-1 – Luc Montagnier *(Courtesy Pasteur Institute)*

that the African virus was only about 40 percent homologous with the original HIV virus, but was closely related to the immunodeficiency virus isolated by Harvard researchers in 1985 from masque monkeys at the New England Primate Center.

For obvious reasons, a vaccine against AIDS has become a major research priority at the Pasteur Institute.

With regard to relatively recent research, there have been other important highlights. For instance:

A kit for use in the diagnosis and follow-up of colonic and rectal cancer has been devised. It works on the principle that a compound called villin, characteristically found in the epithelial cells of the intestinal tract, is present in the blood in some malignancies of the colon and rectum.

A new genetically engineered vaccine against hepatitis B has been marketed under the name Gen Hevac D.

The genome of an isolate of Hepatitis C (from a resident of the United States) was cloned and sequenced.

Fibronectin, a protein that binds reversibly to the external face of the plasma membrane has been studied. These studies have shown that neoplastic cells are deficient in this protein, and this has led to the speculation that fibronectin deficiency could be associated with the property of invasion — a property that characterizes malignancy.

A detailed study of the structure and action of some of the toxins contained in snake venoms has been conducted. The object of this investigation is to improve the efficacy of antivenom treatments.

It has been determined that the agent of Lyme disease consists of at least three varieties: one (a United States variety) is responsible for arthritis; others are more prone to promote neurological or delayed cutaneous reactions.

The course of the cholera pandemic of the 1990's was followed. The arrival of the disease at Santo Domingo, Dominican Republic, was anticipated, and a successful strategy to prevent an epidemic there was implemented.

A diagnostic polymerase chain reaction method was instituted for some chlamydia and for the agent of Q fever, both of which require special methods for growth.

The concept of apoptosis, or programmed cell death, was studied. Since some lymphocytes from people with HIV-positive blood die in cell culture, there is a possibility that this phenomenon may have important implications with regard to the destruction of T-helper lymphocytes. This destruction is an important factor in making AIDS lethal.

Maxime Schwartz, Director of the Pasteur Institute, made this observation about its research: "Whatever the origin of their subject, be it historic or recent, scientists at the Institut Pasteur take care to balance the fundamental and applied aspects of their work."

Today, the Institute has a large campus encompassing many buildings. For example, the Department of Immunology is housed in, appropriately, the Metchnikoff Building, and the Department of Molecular Biology in the Jacques Monod Building. The Institute employs a staff of some 2,300 people. One thousand of these are permanent scientists paid by the Pasteur Institute or by public agencies. There are also numerous visiting scientists from many different nations who have access to the latest technology.

Financial support breaks down as follows:

Government	47%
Own resources	29%
Industrial royalties	10%
Private support	14%

With regard to the last item, the late Duchess of Windsor contributed by willing her jewels.

The Hospital of the Pasteur Institute, established for clinical research, has 65 beds. It provides consultations for infectious and allergic diseases and has a center for specialized information and vaccinations for travelers to the tropics. Currently, about three-quarters of the inpatients and about half of the outpatients are infected with AIDS.

The Institute is also an advanced level teaching center for scientists and physicians from around the globe. In addition, it functions as a worldwide epidemiological screening unit, working for the French government and WHO (World Health Organization).

Overseas, the Institute has a network of affiliates oriented toward medical and health problems that affect developing countries.

A merger of the Institut Merieux, Pasteur Vaccins, and Canada's Connought firm made Pasteur-Merieux Serums and Pasteur Vaccins the largest vaccine producer in the world.

Figure 10-2 — A building of the Pasteur Institute campus.
(Courtesy Pasteur Institute)

Research done at the Institute embraces many areas of health and industry, with the greatest emphasis on public health. Currently, the larger department are divided as follows:

BACTERIOLOGY AND MYCOLOGY — Here there is emphasis on diagnosis and epidemiological studies. The department maintains collections of strains and plays a major role in France's public health service. Research centers on the treatment of opportunistic fungal infections.

ECOLOGY — The work here is oriented toward such projects as control of tropical disease vectors and combatting arborviruses (i.e. arthropod-borne viruses). The aim is not to eradicate one species in relation to another, but to find a state of equilibrium compatible with living organisms and innocuous to humans and the beneficial fauna. Studies include various types of resistance in parasites and vectors.

INTERNATIONAL PASTEUR INSTITUTES
AND ASSOCIATED INSTITUTES - 1992

Pasteur Institute of Algeria

Pasteur Institute of Bangui, Central African Republic

Pasteur Institute of the Ivory Coast, Abidian

Pasteur Institute of Dakar, Senegal

Pasteur Institue of Guadeloupe, Pointe-à-Pitre

Pasteur Institute of French Guiana, Cayenne

Greek Pasteur Institute, Athens

Pasteur Institute of Ho Chi Minh Ville, Vietnam

Pasteur Institute of Iran, Teheran

Pasteur Institute of Lille, France

Pasteur Institute of Lyon, France

Pasteur Institute of Madagascar, Tenanarive

Pasteur Institute of Morocco, Casablanca

Pasteur Institute of Nhatrang, Vietnam

Pasteur Institute of New Caledonia, Noumea

Pasteur Institute of Phnom-Penh, Cambodia

Pasteur Institute of Rome, Italy

Pasteur Institute of Tunis, Tunisia

Pasteur Center of Cameroon, Yaounde

Bolivian Institute of Altitude Biology, La Paz

Cantachuzeme Institute, Bucharest

National Institute of Hygiene and Epidemiology of Hanoi, Vietnam

Institute of Research and Applied Biology of Guinea, Kindia

Territorial Medical Research Institute Louis Malarde, Papeete, French
Polynesia

National Laboratory of Public Health, Brazzaville, Congo

VIROLOGY – There is concentration on viruses that cause major human and veterinary diseases. The general research themes are concerned with the mechanisms of viral expression, the physiopathology of certain viral diseases, and the relationship of some viruses with human cancers. Papilloma viruses (those which cause warts) are used as a model for the latter. Applied research is aimed at diagnosis and its application to epidemiology. New approaches to vaccine development are evaluated.

IMMUNOLOGY – The goal of this department is the biological understanding of individuality and of the mechanisms that allow vertebrates to identify, recognize, and remember their antigenic experiences in molecular terms. With regard to antigen and antibodies, there is concentration on the identification or recognition of molecular shapes. This recognition is based on physicochemical complementarity.

BIOCHEMISTRY AND MOLECULAR GENETICS – The main categories of study are chemical and biochemical molecules of medical and industrial use, the identification of new tumor markers, and the analysis of cells or their components.

MOLECULAR BIOLOGY – Most of this department's research is focused on questions of biological regulation – at the level of molecular interactions, cell differentiation, or embryological development. Gene sequencing is an important function, and the department participates in the European Project of sequencing the yeast genome.

EXPERIMENTAL PHYSIOPATHOLOGY – Here are analyzed secondary responses to pathogens and inflammatory agents such as snake venom. This is done at levels ranging from the whole organism to the molecule.

BIOTECHNOLOGY – This division embraces fundamental and applied microbiology, gene structure and function, and neurobiology. There is a focus on hereditary sensory defects that occur in man. Antibodies raised against many different antigens are prepared and provided.

AIDS AND RETROVIRUSES – The scientific projects are oriented chiefly toward HIV and AIDS. In addition, there are projects that involve disease models for multiple sclerosis, epidemiological studies of HTLV-I, and utilization of retroviral vectors for gene therapy.

MEDICINE – This department includes the Hospital of the Pasteur Institute, the Blood Transfusion Center, and the Immuno-Allergy Unit.

In 1988, the complete nucleotide sequence of the rabies virus was determined at the Pasteur Institute. This exemplifies how the state of knowledge has continued to advance since Pasteur's day, when he lacked the technical means even to see that virus. At the same time, the research aims of the Institute are in accord with its founder's philosophy.

Chapter 11

AIDS

Between September, 1980, and May, 1981, the United States Centers for Disease Control (now CDCP) in Atlanta had five requests for pentamidine iso-ethionate, an experimental drug used to treat a rare type of pneumonia caused by the protozoan *Pneumocystis carinii*. Most cases of this type arise in persons who are taking drugs to depress the immune system. These patients, however, did not fit this category; they were all homosexual males living in Los Angeles.

In a 23-month period before that, there had been only two such requests for patients not taking immunosuppressive drugs. Sandra Ford, the technician responsible for processing rare drug orders, brought this increase in requests to the attention of her superiors. In June, 1981, the CDC's newsletter noted the unusual cases.

That same year there were reports of an increased incidence of Kaposi's sarcoma occurring in homosexual men in New York and California. Kaposi's sarcoma is a rare type of tumor, usually seen first as a skin lesion that spreads to various parts of the body. Some of the victims also had *Pneumocystis carinii* pneumonia and other infections due to yeast, herpes virus, cytomegalovirus, and other organisms.

When 1982 ended, it was known that the syndrome called AIDS could affect, besides homosexuals, intravenous drug users as well as recipients of blood transfusions and Factor VIII, a plasma concentrate used to treat hemophilia. These facts pointed to an infectious agent present in blood and semen. In its preparation, Factor VIII is passed through a filter that holds back fungi and bacteria, so there was a possibility that a virus was the culprit.

One investigator, vitally interested in the identification of this agent, was physician-virologist Robert Gallo of the National Institutes of Health in Bethesda, Maryland. In 1978, as previously noted, his team had discovered the first human retrovirus. Named HTLV-I, it caused a type of leukemia seen in Japan and central Africa, among other locales. Gallo also headed the group that first isolated HTLV-II, the cause of a rare disease known as hairy-cell leukemia. These two diseases are characterized by a proliferation of T-helper cells, sometimes called CD4 lymphocytes for the antigen they carry.

AIDS, on the other hand, is characterized by a destruction of T-helper lymphocytes. There were, however, similarities between the disease processes caused by the HTLV and the AIDS agent and, in the spring of 1982, Gallo proposed that the cause of AIDS was likely to be a new human retrovirus.

To isolate HTLV-I, Gallo's group used a culture of T cells stimulated by a growth factor named Interleukin-II. To identify the virus, he depended on a sensitive assay for reverse transcriptase and visualization with the electron microscope. He now followed the same procedure to identify the virus responsible for AIDS, a putative retrovirus. He began work late in 1982, using tissue from people with AIDS. In the fall of 1983, Mikulas Popovic, a member of Gallo's

Figure 11-1 – Robert Gallo *(Courtesy National Institutes of Health)*

team, found a clone of leukemia cells that provided a way to culture the virus in quantities sufficient for antibody testing.

Thus, it became possible to examine stored samples isolated from suspected cases – in other words, epidemiological data could be obtained. This infected line, H9, was given to several biotechnical concerns so there could be commercial development of an antibody test. Such a test was available in 1985, and the risk of further spreading of AIDS through blood transfusions and blood products was greatly reduced in the United States.

Gallo's group published their results in May, 1984. This post-dated the Pasteur Institute's first paper on AIDS. The American group reported that a new retrovirus, which they named HTLV-III, was the cause of AIDS.

In 1988, Peter Duesberg, professor of molecular biology at the University of California in Berkeley, challenged the assumption that HIV, as it is now named, causes AIDS, mainly because it had not yet met all of Koch's Postulates. (Reproducing the disease in animals has been difficult, and ethical considerations of course preclude infecting humans.)

Here is the chief thrust of the argument advanced by Gallo and colleagues:

> The strongest evidence that HIV causes AIDS comes from prospective epidemiological studies that document the absolute requirement for HIV infection for the development of AIDS. It has been shown for every population group studied in the United States and elsewhere that, in the years following the introduction of HIV and subsequent seroconversion of members of that population, the features characteristic of progressive immunodeficiency emerge in a predictable sequence resulting in clinical AIDS.

An unfortunate dispute arose between the two AIDS research teams over patents for diagnostic tests. The Pasteur Institute claimed that Gallo's group had used the Pasteur virus to develop an antibody test. (Montagnier had sent Gallo material with the specification that the virus was not to be used for commercial purposes.) There was also controversy about who discovered the AIDS virus.

The Pasteur Institute brought suit to overturn the American patent granted to Gallo. Since the Pastorians had filed first, they believed they were treated unfairly. (On the other hand, their method of cell culture was less efficient than that of the Gallo team.)

The matter was resolved in 1987 without going to court and with the pledge that all pending suits would be dropped. It was also agreed to create an AIDS foundation financed by 80 percent of the antibody test royalties that both the Institute and the United States government receive between 1987 and 2002. When definitive tests proved that LAV-I and HTLV-III were very similar, the names HIV-I, II, III, etc., proposed by an international committee, were accepted, and they were classified as lentiviruses. There was also agreement that the discovery of HIV was a joint endeavor of Gallo and Montagnier and their co-workers.

The patent disagreement surfaced again when Gallo conceded in 1991 that, due to contamination, his lab was working with the French virus when the American diagnostic test was developed. Maxime Schwartz contended that the Pasteur Institute, which he heads, should receive the bulk of the millions of dollars earned annually in royalties for the test. Gallo's position has been that his ground work made possible the success of Montagnier's group in developing a satisfactory test, and that it matters little whose virus was used.

Gallo has noted that never has so much been learned about a disease in so short a time as was learned about AIDS between 1982 and 1984. "Without the tools of molecular biology we could never have moved so fast," he once said in an interview. He believes that the competition between his team and Montagnier's accelerated the pace of research.

The AIDS virus has been described as the most intensively studied one in history. Electron microscopy has shown that the HIV virion, or particle, is an icosahedron, covered with a lipid bilayer membrane. Projecting from this membrane are numerous knobs composed of glycoprotein (gp), a combination of protein with a sugar (figure 12-1). Each knob has three sets of protein molecules (figure 12-2). The viral core includes glycoproteins and proteins (p) as well as RNA and the pivotal enzyme, reverse transcriptase. Binding takes place between the viral envelope GP 120 and CD4 receptors present primarily on T-helper cells. The GP 41 also enters into the fusion process.

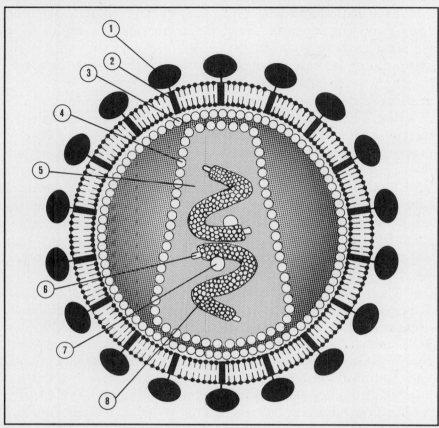

Figure 12-1 – HIV virion in cross section. (1) GP 120 (2) GP 41 (3) P 17/18 (4) P 24/25 (5) Core (6) RNA (7) Reverse transcriptase (8) P9, P7

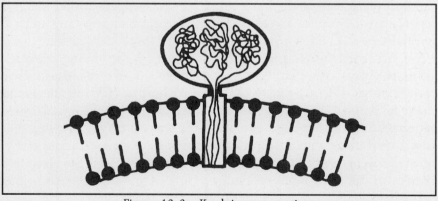

Figure 12-2 – Knob in cross section.

The virus enters T-helper lymphocytes and replicates. Macrophages/monocytes and certain structures in the lymph nodes also entrap the particles in the same fashion. A later discovery showed that HIV exists in large amounts in lymphoid tissue associated with the gut and in lymph nodes throughout the body. HIV is found in brain tissue, possibly carried there by macrophages.

The T-helper lymphocytes secrete protein factors that stimulate various other cells that participate in the immune response. Some of the secreted factors cause B-lymphocytes to produce antibodies. Normally, people have a 2:1 ratio of T-helper to T-killer lymphocytes. (The T-killer cells are cytotoxic.) People infected with HIV ultimately have a reversed ratio, because the T-helper cells die as viral replication progresses. The loss of T-helper lymphocytes is disastrous because it encourages infections that may be lethal. Such infections are due to various organisms, including some that ordinarily would not be pathogenic, referred to as opportunistic.

The absolute T-helper cell count is a prognostic sign in AIDS. The normal value is 800 to 1,000 T-helper cells per cubic millimeter of blood. Carriers without symptoms have around 200 to 500. Some AIDS patients have no cells that can be detected. It is now possible to enumerate both T-helper and T-killer cells with an automatic counter. They are distinguished by their specific antibodies. The death of infected lymphocytes is characterized by the formation of syncytia, great multinuclear cells that result from the fusion of many individual cells.

An average of about nine years passes between the time the blood becomes positive and the patient exhibits the full blown clinical disease of AIDS. Some investigators believe that a co-factor or co-factors may operate to bring about the viral change from latency to activity.

Epidemiological and sequencing data have led some investigators to speculate that HIV-I and HIV-II arose in Africa from retroviruses affecting monkeys. The first human HIV infections may have taken place more than 20 but less than 100 years ago. Estimates are based on the expected rate of evolutionary change per generation for a viral nucleotide sequence when subjected to a different sort of environment. Frozen blood samples taken in 1959 from people in Zaire and in 1968 from individuals in the United States have tested positive for HIV-I.

The AIDS virus antigens have even been detected in tissue preserved in blocks of paraffin. A 25-year-old sailor was a patient at the Manchester (England) Royal Infirmary in 1959. He had fever, skin sores, and was wasting away. No treatment helped. An autopsy was done, but the cause of death was not determined. Many years later, when the polymerase chain reaction became available, Manchester virologists were able to identify HIV in specimen blocks.

HIV can infect anyone, including the fetus *in utero*, but homosexual men and intravenous drug users are especially at risk. Gallo stresses that the amount of virus is an important factor in infection. The geographical distribution of the disease knows no bounds. WHO projects a cumulative total of 50 to 40 million HIV infections — in men, women, and children — by the year 2000, 90 percent of them in the developing countries. Estimates such as this are subject to constant revision as new facts emerge.

For those stricken with AIDS, the most urgent need is a drug to control the ravages of the disease, which is currently considered fatal. Various approaches are being tried. One class of drugs that has received much attention is that aimed at undermining reverse transcription. Known as nucleoside analogs, these drugs *fool* the enzyme into using them to make DNA. This results in cessation of the formation of the DNA chain. The drug 3'-azido-deoxy thymidine (AZT) is an example of a nucleoside analog. So far, no drug of this type has proved to be a magic bullet, but research along several avenues continues. There is also some focus on finding effective drugs for specific conditions that occur in patients with AIDS — for example, the meningitis caused by *Cryptococcus*.

No vaccine, either therapeutic or preventive for AIDS, has yet shown evidence of being effective over a prolonged period. Animal models, valuable in testing many vaccines, do not help with AIDS. The HIV virus can be made to multiply in chimpanzee blood, but these animals do not contract the same type of AIDS as humans. In addition, they are considered an endangered species. This means that a new vaccine might have to be tested instead in low-risk volunteers. (High-risk volunteers might have acquired significant immunity). This is one of many obstacles to be overcome.

Scientists in the past have been successful in overcoming formidable obstacles. The story of the Salk poliomyelitis vaccine is an example.

By 1935, two poliomyelitis vaccines had been developed in the United States. Maurice Brodie of New York City used a killed virus vaccine that was given to about 9,000 people. John Kolmer of Philadelphia used an attenuated virus, and his vaccine was given to about 12,000 people. Twelve cases of poliomyelitis, six of them fatal, followed the administration of one or the other of these vaccines. At that point, James Leake, a Public Health Service official, publicly begged Dr. Kolmer to stop using his vaccine, which was made by culturing virus in monkey spinal cords and treating it with phenyl mercury nitrate. Brodie's formalin-killed vaccine was finally judged useless.

In 1949, John Enders and his associates at Harvard Medical School were successful in growing poliomyelitis virus in a culture of kidney cells. This opened they way to large-scale production of the virus. Jonas Salk worked indefatigably to produce a formalin-killed vaccine with three strains of virus. His object was, of course, to preserve adequate antigenicity and, at the same time, produce a safe product. Batches were tried on mice, rabbits, and monkeys. Field trials followed, and, in 1955, Salk was able to announce that his vaccine was 80 to 90 percent effective. In fact, in seven years it reduced the incidence of polio by more than 96 percent. The Sabin oral vaccine followed, and poliomyelitis was conquered.

Publishing only a few weeks after Salk, Jacques Lepine of the Pasteur Institute made a vaccine somewhat similar to Salk's. It was marketed by the Institute starting in 1957 and proved to be totally safe. It was also effective, reducing the incidence of the disease by more than 90 percent.

The experience with polio vaccine reminds us that instant success in science is not the norm; rather, that knowledge builds on prior knowledge, and after much trial and error, a realistic goal can be reached.

In 1988, almost a century after Pasteur's death, Marc Girard, veterinarian and virologist at the Pasteur Institute, commented that one may argue that there is no evidence that a vaccine against AIDS will actually be effective. He noted that there was even greater doubt when Louis Pasteur attempted postexposure vaccination against rabies. And, according to Girard, the success of that and similar attempts "breeds optimism in the belief that a vaccine against AIDS will eventually be found."

Chapter 12

PRESENT DANGERS

The outstanding success of antibiotics, drugs, and vaccines has imparted a sense of unrealistic security. While the means to conquer scores of infectious diseases are at hand, time has shown that eternal vigilance is necessary.

We know, for example, that disease-causing agents undergo genetic change and evolution; we know that their susceptibility to antimicrobial drugs may change. In addition, organisms may infect new hosts or change their response to the host's immunity. Increasingly, the host's immunity may be compromised for various reasons. In the light of such changes, continued research on bacterial and viral mutation, drug resistance, and pesticides is crucial, as are drug development programs and various preventive vaccine programs. In addition, it is important to maintain adequate public health measures and, if necessary, extend them. Environmental changes due to the development of rural areas and to the movement of people and products from remote to populous areas present potential dangers.

In 1991, because of the neglect of these and other matters, a 19-member multi-disciplinary committee of authorities began a 16-month study of emerging microbial threats to health. Working under the auspices of the National Research Council (USA), the members of the project published their results and recommendations in *Emerging Infections: Microbial Threats to Health in the United States*. The brief accounts that follow are a few examples of diseases that have emerged or reemerged recently.

PLAGUE

For centuries, plague has been a scourge of mankind, causing extreme suffering and countless deaths. Three major epidemics have been recorded, most notable of which was the Black Death (1346 to 1361). The Black Death derived it name from the hemorrhage of the skin and internal organs, which turn dark or even black.

Some historians now believe that the Black Death may have begun in the area of the Caspian Sea. In 1346, many Taters in the Crimea contracted bubonic plague, so called because of the characteristic *bubo*, a lymph gland enlarged by an inflammatory process. Before 1346, there were only occasional outbreaks of the human form, and it is speculated that until then, *Yersinia pestis*, the causative organism, spread slowly in the rodent population. (We recall that the pathogen was discovered by the Pasteur Institute's Alexandre Yersin.)

It is now known that one habitat of *Yersinia pestis* is the bloodstream of rats. The organism multiplies rapidly when the disease becomes epizootic; what causes the change from the enzootic to epizootic state is not clear. A vector, commonly the rat flea, transfers the bacillus to other rats and to humans. The insect lives in the rat's fur. After biting its host, the flea draws both blood and bacilli into its own stomach where the organisms reproduce and are eventually regurgitated by the surfeited flea when it attempts to feed again. Feces from the flea are often introduced through minute cuts in the skin. *Yersinia* organisms soon kill the rat. (The abrupt appearance of dead or dying rats is associated with the beginning of an epidemic.) Modern epidemiologists stress that when plague is epizootic and the affected animals have close proximity to humans, epidemics are likely to occur.

In the case of the Black Death, shipborn rats and fleas spread the disease to Sicily and Italy via the commercial routes of the day. From Sicily, plague was introduced to northern Africa, Sardinia, Corsica, and Spain. From Venice and other Italian cities, it spread to France and Germany, among other countries. Venice codified the first systematic quarantine policy on March 20, 1348, closing that port for 40 days to all travelers and ships suspected of harboring the disease. Plague reached Moscow via western Europe and the Hanseatic League ports. As the disease progressed, some victims developed the lethal pneumonic form of plague. In this type, bacteria enter the lung.

Expelled droplets thus become highly contagious, providing a means of person-to-person infection. It is estimated that a least a quarter of Europe's population succumbed to the Black Death.

Although the disease of plague is rare in modern times, much epidemiological knowledge can be learned from its history. Important to note is the fact that plague infection is currently enzootic in many rodents in the western United States, Mexico, and Canada.

TUBERCULOSIS

Tuberculosis, another bacterial disease with very low prevalence for several decades, has since 1985 again become a serious threat. More than 26,000 new cases with 1,700 related deaths occur annually in the United States. It is estimated that ten million people in the United States are infected; some will never have clinical symptoms, but others will develop the disease. Sybil Wellstood of the U. S. Food and Drug Administration lists some of the factors responsible for the resurgence of this disease, only recently considered *historic*.

- Increased poverty and homelessness
- Crowded living conditions in group home settings and prisons
- Drug abuse
- HIV infections
- Immigrants from countries with a high prevalence of disease
- Treatment failures
- Failure to prevent disease transmission related to inadequate infection control practices and isolation facilities in institutions
- Insufficient federal and state funding for tuberculosis prevention and control programs

Treatment failures are related to the development of drug resistance, and a small number of cases are fatal because they do not respond to any antituberculosis drug.

Frank Ryan's book, *The Forgotten Plague*, traces the arduous route to the conquest of tuberculosis. He also points out how the disease is reemerging in the 1990's.

In the past, the laboratory diagnosis and surveillance of tuberculosis by conventional methods has been difficult because the organism takes so long to grow. Fortunately, several sophisticated rapid diagnostic techniques are now available.

GROUP A STREPTOCOCCUS

Group A streptococci may cause serious diseases, among them scarlet fever, rheumatic fever, erysipelas, septicemia, and puerperal sepsis. These disorders have not been common for many years, but before the advent of sulfanilamide and penicillin, a skin cut could be fatal if a Group A streptococcus were introduced into the blood stream. In 1924, Calvin Coolidge, Jr., son of the 30th president, died of a streptococcal infection resulting from an infected blister.

As late as 1989, there were reports of deaths due to a Group A streptococcus. Some investigators believe that the pathogen involved is not new; others are convinced that this highly virulent organism is the result of a recent mutation.

LISTEROSIS

Listerosis is caused by *Listeria monocytogenes*. This bacterium was discovered in 1928. At first, the incidence of the disease was low; in 1960, only 50 cases were reported worldwide. But in 1982, this figure had reached 10,000.

Listerosis is sometimes seen in pregnant women or their newborn offspring. It also is more likely to appear in immunosuppressed individuals than in those with normally functioning immune systems. The victim's immune system may be weakened by inherited diseases, prematurity in neonates, pregnancy, other concurrent infections, aging, or malignancy, to name a few. Other promoting factors may be man-made interventions such as chemotherapy for neoplastic disease, transplantation medication, treatment for autoimmune disease, and radiation. In human listerosis, there may be meningoencephalitis and/or septicemia resulting in death. The pathogen is transmitted mainly in contaminated food that has not been sufficiently heated. Hot dogs, chicken, and various soft cheeses have been implicated.

INFLUENZA

The influenza pandemic of 1918 ranks among the most devastating disasters in human history; in less that 12 months, it took more than 20 million lives. The virus was not isolated, so it cannot be subjected to the tools of modern molecular biology – tools that could provide much useful information. Nevertheless, serological findings* offer considerable confidence that a virus, antigenically similar to the one that caused the great pandemic of 1918, exists today in swine. Identified as influenza A, it has been shown to be the cause of additional major worldwide epidemics in 1957 and 1968. These outbreaks were due to the emergence of completely new subtypes of the virus – a process known as antigenic shift – that carried significant mutations. These may result from an exchange of nucleic acid between two viruses infecting the pig – one an avian influenza virus and the other a human influenza virus.

Minor antigenic changes – antigenic drift – are responsible for annual epidemic and regional outbreaks. Thus, constant changes in the composition of influenza A vaccine are necessary.

With regard to influenza (and some other diseases), an observation of Joshua Lederberg, 1959 Nobel Laureate, is germane: "Pandemics are not acts of God but are built into the ecologic relations between viruses, animal species, and the human species."

DENGUE

Dengue fever, which commonly affects young children, has been seen in tropical climates for centuries. Four serotypes have been discovered; primary infection with any one of them causes the disease. A more severe form, dengue hemorrhagic fever/dengue shock syndrome (DHF/DSS), is a product of the 20th century, first recognized in epidemic form in Manila in 1953. It occurs when the patient has been infected with two or more serotypes.

The causative organism, classified as an arbovirus, is transmitted by the bite of an infected *Aedes aegypti* or *Aedes albopictus* mosquito. The disease is epidemic and endemic in tropical and subtropical

---

*Laboratories of the Pasteur Institute, CDPC, and elsewhere maintain collections of blood sera (that contain antibodies) and cultures of organisms isolated from epidemics. These may by used as references when new epidemics or puzzling sporadic cases are being investigated.

areas of Africa, the Americas, Asia, Oceania, and Australia; and is widespread in the Caribbean basin.

Worldwide, there has been a large increase in DHF/DSS since the 1950's, attributed to a lack of effective mosquito control, increased urbanization in the tropics, and increased air travel. The more recent vector, *Aedes albopictus* (known as the Asian tiger mosquito), was introduced into the United States in used tires imported from Japan. The tires collect rain water, making suitable pools for breeding.

The four serotypes have made vaccine development difficult. Workers at the Pasteur Institute of New Caledonia have joined with other scientists in producing a method that identifies the serotype(s) present. Work on the vaccine is progressing.

INFECTIONS WITH FILOVIRUSES

In the late 1960's, African green monkeys from Uganda were sent to Marburg, Germany, for a vaccine project. Some of the animals became sick and died; people who had handled the animals died and there were secondary infections with a very serious febrile disease. The causative agent was a virus that came to be named Marburg.

In the 1970's, three separate epidemics in Africa were due to Ebola virus. Named for a river in Zaire, it causes a greatly feared hemorrhagic disease in humans.

In 1989, viral infection appeared in cynomolgus monkeys shipped from the Philippines to the CDC unit in Reston, Virginia, to be used in medical research. Subsequent study showed that a virus – later named Reston – was responsible. Reston appeared not to be a threat to human life.

These three viruses are now classified as filoviruses. Since there is no effective treatment, extreme caution in handling these and other new types of lethal microorganisms is necessary. Since 1985, the Pasteur Institute has had a high security laboratory for such study.

In 1993, a lethal infection appeared suddenly among people living on or near a Navajo Indian reservation, which includes parts of New Mexico, Arizona, and Utah. The first case of the deadly, flu-like respiratory illness occurred on March 8, 1993. Officials from state health departments and the CDCP investigated and, three months later, the causative agent was identified as a hantavirus (figure 12-1).

These are only a few samples of *emerging viruses*. Stephen Morse, an eminent virologist, emphasizes that usually what causes these unwelcome emergences is some human activity that brings about the transfer of viruses to new hosts. Donald Henderson, a public health specialist, notes that more progress toward control might be made if scientists applied what is already known.

In December, 1890, two years after the founding of the Pasteur Institute, a young doctor in the French Navy had just completed a novel course at the Institute. It was called *Microbie technique* and was under the direction of Roux. The student was Albert Calmette, then 27, and he was persuaded by Pasteur to create the first overseas affiliate of the Pasteur Institute in Saigon. The facility he founded is

Fatal virus is present everywhere

NEW YORK (AP) – The family of viruses responsible for the mystery disease that has killed 16 people in the Southwest is found in rats in cities around the world, and could strike humans anywhere, a researcher said Thursday.

Because the virus does not spread from one person to another, these outbreaks can be contained by controlling rodent populations. said virologist Stephen S. Morse of The Rockefeller University in New York.

Also Thursday, the U.S. Centers for Disease Control and Prevention reported finding genetic material from a newly recognized rodent virus in two victims, meaning that the virus almost certainly caused the deaths.

The officials also reported that three people in the Southwest had been infected with the virus in 1991 and 1992.

The virus is a member of the family called hantaviruses, named for the Hantaan River in Korea, where the first one was discovered.

Figure 12-1 – Associated Press release of July 17, 1993

known today as Institut Pasteur de Ho Chi Minh Ville. It is one of many such facilities that are linked to the mother institution in Paris. They are well equipped to face the everpresent problems that involve human and animal health. The fact that Pasteur encouraged a global outlook is another example of his wisdom and continuing influence.

On the occasion of his 70th birthday, Louis Pasteur said this in an address: "...whether our efforts are or are not favored by life, let us be able to say, when we come near the great goal, 'I have done what I could.'"

Pasteur's *could* changed history.

APPENDIX A

The following was written by the author in 1973 for *People & Places,* a Great Lakes regional magazine. The names have been changed to protect privacy; the dialogue is invented. The rest is factual, and demonstrates the importance of the sulfa drug at the time.

DAUGHTER OF JAIRUS

She lay there as if asleep, her curly black hair accentuating the whiteness of the hospital pillowcase. But Bonnie Richards was not asleep — she was unconscious, hovering between this world and the next. A pretty sixteen year old, she had been admitted to the hospital two days previously, and the diagnosis of cerebrospinal meningitis, or spotted fever, was quickly confirmed.

The year was 1940, when doctors had been accustomed to treating the disease with a horse serum containing antibodies that caused some reduction in the mortality figures — but about a third of the cases still died, and many patients were left with serious complications from the disease. Bonnie's doctor decided to try a new treatment that was beginning to show good success — a sulfa drug rather than the usual antiserum therapy.

At the time, I was a medical technologist at the hospital, and it was my duty to make daily analyses of Bonnie's blood and sometimes of her cerebrospinal fluid to determine whether or not the dosage of sulfa was satisfactory. Since Bonnie was in a coma, the medication was given through a stomach tube. The drug was absorbed into the blood from the digestive tract and ultimately reached the cerebrospi-

nal fluid, where it was needed to combat the disease. It was impera-
tive that the sulfa level be kept high enough to ensure an adequate
concentration of the drug in the cerebrospinal fluid; on the other
hand, too high a blood level could cause serious consequences – thus
the necessity of the frequent analyses.

That morning when I went to Bonnie's room to draw samples
for various tests, I thought it would probably be the last time. I had
been there the day before and had thought the same thing then, but
she had lasted another day. As I prepared to leave the room, I spoke to
Bonnie's mother.

"It's only 7:30. You're in early."

"I've stayed in the hospital ever since we brought her here. I stay
in this chair most of the time . . . . My husband comes here right after
work and doesn't leave until ten or so. We have no other children, so
there is no reason for me to be at home. I probably wouldn't get
much sleep there, anyway." She was attired in a mask and an ill-
fitting scrub gown, so I couldn't really see her. But I knew she had
courage and great strength, and my heart went out to her.

When I delivered Bonnie's lab reports, I asked the doctor about
her condition.

"Not good," he said. "This level shows that the drug dosage is
just right, too, but she is still a very sick girl."

The next morning, before starting my blood-collecting, I
checked the list of patients who had died during the night. I had a
psychological block against seeing the room empty – and I felt sure it
would be. But, no, I was wrong; there was no Richards on the list. So
apparently Bonnie was still with us. When I whispered to the special
nurse, "Any change?" she shook her head. Mrs. Richards was still in
the room, reading a book. I thought to myself how much better it
would be if the inevitable were not prolonged; the poor parents
would be spared false hope and much expense.

On the fourth morning, I met the special in one of the elevators.
She was on an errand to the Pharmacy. "I'll see you later," she said
between floors.

"How is she today?" I asked.

"Just the same. Those parents . . . . Such faith and strength! I
dread the thought of being with them when she goes. But I'll cross
that bridge when I get to it."

When I entered Bonnie's room, her mother said, "Good morning," then buried herself in the newspaper. I supposed that she found it distasteful to watch me jab her daughter.

Bonnie seemed different, somehow. When I put a tourniquet on her arm, she moved as if she were conscious. As I withdrew the needle from the vein, I saw a pair of brown eyes gazing at me. The eyelids closed for a moment, then opened again. This time Bonnie spotted the morning paper and her mother.

"Mother, what's the matter with me?"

The newspaper fell to the floor. Mrs. Richards was at the bedside in a moment. "Bonnie! Bonnie! You just spoke to me!"

"Am I very sick?"

"You have been, honey. No, No! Don't try to sit up now!"

"How long is it since I came here?"

"Four days."

"That long! I must have been sick! I'm pretty tired now, and sleepy, but, Mother, I think I'm okay.

"I think so, too. I must call your father. Thank God! Thank God!" cried Mrs. Richards, now weeping.

I was no doctor, but I knew that Bonnie was okay. She was alert; she could hear, speak, and move her legs and arms. There might be a long road ahead, but intuition told me that she was over the hump. I was amazed. It was like seeing the Biblical daughter of Jairus raised from the dead. I got myself out of the room before mother or daughter noticed the tears I could no longer hold back. A miracle drug indeed – this sulfa.

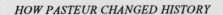

APPENDIX B
THE AGE OF
MOLECULAR BIOLOGY

The relatively new science of molecular biology is concerned with how genes govern cell activity; its purpose is the interpretation of biological process in terms of interactions between molecules. One scientist was more specific: molecular biology is the study of structure, function, and biogenesis of nucleic acids and proteins.

Before 1944, many scientists thought that proteins, rather than DNA, were the carriers of genetic information. This idea was proven incorrect by Oswald Avery, Colin McLeod, and Maclyn McCarty of the Rockefeller Institute for Medical Research.* Using *Streptococcus pneumoniae*, they showed conclusively that the genetic material was deoxyribonucleic acid (DNA). Although their work did not immediately receive the attention it merited, it was confirmed, and scientists accepted the fact that DNA is the material that controls life – the material of which the chromosomes are composed.

By 1950, the chemical composition of DNA had been worked out. The basic unit, known as a nucleotide, is made up of a phosphate group and a sugar called deoxyribose. The sugar may be attached to any of four bases – adenine (A), guanine (G), cytosine (C), or thymine (T).

---

*Opened in 1904, this developed into one of the principal research organizations in the United States.

The master molecule turned out to have a complex structure. In 1953, James Watson, an American, and Francis Crick of England produced a molecular model which corresponded with the X-ray diffraction pattern of DNA. They correctly envisioned the DNA molecule as being composed of two strands twisted together about each other in opposite directions to form a double helix. (Imagine a helix as a coil of wire.) The phosphate-sugar backbone is outside, with the bases in the center of the coil. The bases of the two chains always pair in a predicted manner: A with T and G with C. A is said to be complementary to T and G complementary to C. The two strands of the molecule are held together by a special type of bonding (hydrogen bonds) between the AT and GC pairs. Since the bonds between the bases are relatively weak, when the two strands of the double helix separate during replication, the hydrogen bonds split, but the individual strands of sugar-phosphate backbone with the attached bases remain intact.

The Watson-Crick double-helix model provided, for the first time, a logical explanation of why, by cell division, the daughter cells are identical to the parent cell*. The model also became the keystone of molecular biology. In a relatively short time, thousands of investigators were determining the sequence of animal, plant, bacterial, and viral genes and of the chemical and conformational structure of proteins, as well. The structure of antibodies was being revealed.

Long folded chains of repetitive DNA molecules constitute the chromosomes of the cell's nucleus. (There are 23 pairs in man.) The genes consist of sequences within the much larger chromosomes. Estimates place the number of genes in the human genome between 50,000 and 100,000; many of these have not as yet been fully identified.

Ribonucleic acid (RNA) has only one strand and its sugar is ribose rather than deoxyribose. The bases are A, G, and C, as in DNA, but the C is paired with a base called uracil (U) instead of the very similar T. Most viruses have DNA, but some have only RNA. RNA plays a crucial role in protein synthesis.

DNA and RNA are informational molecules whose complexity underlies the complexity of living organisms. The information

---

*There are exceptions due to factors that cause breakage of the strands or errors in copying. The change, a spontaneous mutation, is passed on to succeeding generations if the change is compatible with survival. Mutations can be induced by irradiation with X-rays or ultraviolet light and by other means.

resides in the linear sequence of the bases. In mitotic cell division, the DNA double helix splits into two strands, each of which serves as a template for the assembly of a complementary strand. This results in two daughter double helixes identical to the parent molecule which may be passed to the daughter cells. Between cell divisions, the DNA may similarly code the sequences of RNA molecules, which are, in turn, involved in protein synthesis. The messenger RNA (mRNA), in particular, codes the sequence of amino acids in a complex protein molecule – each amino acid being determined by a sequence of three bases of the RNA. (Twenty amino acids are the building blocks of proteins. Examples of proteins include contractile proteins of muscle, collagen fibers, hemoglobin, almost all enzymes, and some hormones.) Two other forms of RNA are involved in protein synthesis. Transfer RNA (tRNA) molecules join to specific amino acids and transfer the amino acid into a growing protein molecule. Ribosomal RNA (rRNA) forms the structure of the ribosomes, the site of protein synthesis. All these reactions are mediated by cellular enzyme systems. The proteins of the cell – particularly the enzymes – are the principle determinants of cellular capabilities.

The relationship between the base sequences of DNA and the amino acid sequences of proteins is called the *genetic code*. Although there are minor differences in details, the fundamental process of replication (DNA synthesis), transcription (DNA to RNA), and translation (RNA to protein) occur in all organisms. The genetic code is universal, meaning that the same sequence of these bases determines the same amino acid in the proteins of all living organisms. Jacques Monod noted that what applies to *Escherichia coli* also applies to an elephant.

Mistakes in DNA replication yield mutations. To illustrate, a mutation can cause a substitution of one amino acid for another (e.g., valine for glutamic acid) at a specific location in the hemoglobin molecule. The result is a devastating hereditary disease known as sickle cell anemia, caused by an abnormal hemoglobin. Not all mutations are so harmful.

By 1968, the complete amino acid sequence of an antibody had been found. The sites of recognition bind to very specific sites on the surface of an antigen. These sites are usually composed of protein or carbohydrate that is part of a bacterium or other organism. Monoclonal antibodies are made from a single hybridoma cell formed by the fusion of a specific antibody-manufacturing cell (plasma cell) with a myeloma cell. Since the latter cell is neoplastic, the hybrid cell proliferates without limit, producing a desired amount of antibody. Enzyme-linked immunosorbent assay (ELISA) is a sensitive and useful method for measuring protein. It uses *pure* antibody.

Radioactive isotopes are beneficial by-products of the atomic bomb project. These tracer substances emit particles that may be measured. Radioactive tracers are especially useful when it is desired to know whether compound X is transformed to compound Y in a given system. To do this, compound Y is isolated and purified. A determination of its radioactivity would show whether or not the incorporation has taken place. An example of a radioactive isotope is S^{35}. The superscript is the atomic weight of the radioactive sulfur. When S^{35} is incorporated into the sulfur-containing amino acid methionine, for example, the resulting radioactive methionine is referred to as labeled or tagged. The activity of the label is obtained in various ways: one is by autoradiography, a process whereby the labeled substance is overlaid with a photographic emulsion sensitive to radiation.

The polymerase chain reaction (PCR) is an enzymatic method of producing large amounts of specific DNA, or its fragments, from minute amounts. Among many uses, it is valuable in detecting, with relative speed, such organisms as *Mycobacterium tuberculosis* and *Borrelia burgdorferi* or viruses, all of which grow slowly with conventional culture methods.

Restriction enzymes were discovered by Werner Arber of Switzerland and by Hamilton Smith and Daniel Nathans of the United States. Sometimes called restriction endonucleases, these enzymes are extremely useful in splitting DNA into specific fragments. Hundreds of these enzymes are now known.

Electrophoresis is a process whereby substances may be separated on the basis of their differing electrical charges. This causes them to migrate at different rates when an electric current is passed through. Electrophoresis may be done in various media, including gels.

Molecular hybridization is used to identify DNA structure. Since heating will cause the double strands of DNA to separate, tagged (radioactive or identifiable by other means) probes of known composition can be used to combine with the single-strand DNA if the base sequences of the two are complementary. This will determine, for example, whether or not a nucleic acid of unknown composition is similar to that of a known probe.

An elegant technique known as *Southern blotting* (for E. M. Southern, the scientist from the United Kingdom who originated it) uses many of these methods to demonstrate small differences between related molecules. Electrophoresis separates a mixture of restriction fragments. Single-stranded DNA is created by denaturation and the fragments transferred by *blotting* to a nitrocellulose sheet, with preservation of their position in the gel. They are then hybridized with a single-stranded DNA probe, which is labeled with P^{32}. When a restriction fragment has a sequence complementary to the radioactive probe, autoradiography will point it out. (A similar process for RNA is called *Northern blotting*. When the process is used to identify a protein by means of an antigen-antibody reaction, the procedure is called *Western blotting*.)

Recombinant DNA technology makes possible new combinations of unrelated genes. A given DNA fragment is joined to, for example, plasmids or a phage. The latter are named vectors. *Escherichia coli* is often used as the host cell for the phage. Cells with recombinant DNA — from that of both the host and the introduced DNA — are then cloned. This technology is widely used for vaccine production and for the synthesis of important DNA-determined products such as insulin and growth hormone.

Nuclear magnetic resonance (NMR) is a process whereby the physical structure of such macromolecules as antigen-antibody complexes can be studied.

Gene therapy uses recombinant DNA technology to splice normal genes into the somatic cells of a child bearing a genetic defect. This has been done for a few conditions, of which cystic fibrosis is one. Another is a type of immune deficiency disease in which an essential enzyme is lacking, allowing for the accumulation of toxic substances that destroy T cells. To prevent this from becoming lethal, T cells are removed from the patient. They are then exposed to a retrovirus made harmless and used as a vector to carry the missing gene (which has been transferred to the virus) into the T cell's nucleus. Culture of the doctored T cells produces large numbers of healthy T cells that may be introduced into the child's circulation.

The treatment must be repeated every six months, since it does not affect germ cells.

The techniques noted here have influenced laboratories throughout the world; some have even brought Nobel Prizes to their originators; some, such as sequencing for DNA, lend themselves to automation and are used commercially. Concepts are extremely important – usually more so than techniques, but technology cannot be downgraded. It is instructive to know that even after insulin was discovered, little progress was made against diabetes mellitus until the hormone could be mass produced. And, although the properties of penicillin were known, it contributed little to the control of infection until commercial production became a reality.

More recently, the gene which produces silk in the Golden Orb weaver spider has been isolated and inserted into a bacterium to produce an inexpensive fiber stronger than the silk from the silkworm. It is interesting to speculate about how Pasteur, who saved France's sericulture industry, would have reacted to this feat of biotechnology. Surely he would have been intrigued by the whole process, and especially that microbes, which occupied so much of his attention, were involved.

REFERENCES

Ackerknecht, E. H. 1982. *A Short History of Medicine*, rev. ed. Baltimore: Hopkins.

American Cancer Society. *1988. The Cell: Structure and Function.* New York.

Anderson, C. 1993. Pasteur Notebooks Reveal Deception. *Science,* 259: 1117.

Angert, R. *et al.* 1993. The Largest Bacterium. *Nature,* 362: 239-41.

Applequist, J. 1987. *Am. Scientist,* 75, #1, 63.

Aron, R. *1964. France Reborn. The History of the Liberation.* New York: Scribner's.

Asimov, I. *1982. Asimov's Biographical Encyclopedia of Science and Technology.* Garden City, NY: Doubleday.

Barré-Sinoussi, F. *et al.* 1983. Isolation of a T-Lymphotropic Retrovirus from a Patient at Risk for AIDS. *Science,* 220: 868-71.

Baum, R.M. 1993, July 5. AIDS: Scientific Progress, But No Cure in Sight. *Chem. and Eng. News,* 20-27

Denditt, J. 1993. AIDS: The Unanswered Question. *Science,* 260:1253-93.

Beveridge, W.I.B. 1977. *Influenza, The Last Great Plague.* New York: Prodist.

Beveridge, W.I.B. *1980. Seeds of Discovery.* New York: Norton.

Bigley, N. *1975. Immunological Fundamentals.* Chicago: Year Book.

Blattner, W. *et al.* 1988. HIV Causes AIDS. *Science,* 241:515.

Brady, J.C. *et al.* 1989. Cholera: An 18th Century Pathogen Alive and Well in the '80s. *Lab. Med.,* 20:106-8.

Budd, W. *1984. On the Causes of Fever (1839).* D. C. Smith, ed. Baltimore: Hopkins.

Bullock, W. 1938. *The History of Bacteriology.* New York: Oxford. Reprtd. 1960.

Cadeddu, A. 1985. Pasteur et le cholera des poules: revision critique d'un recit historique. *Hist. Phil. Life Sci.,* 7:87-104.

Caldwell, M. *1988. The Last Crusade. The War on Consumption 1862-1954.* New York: Atheneum.

Cartwright, F. C. with Beddings, M. D. *1972. Disease and History.* New York: Dorset.

Crick, F. *1988. What Mad Pursuit: A Personal View of Scientific Discovery.* New York: Basic Books.

Cherfas, J. 1990. Mad Cow Disease: Uncertainty Rules. *Science,* 249: 1492-91.

Colmer, J. and Sodeman, T. M. 1991. Contemporary Pathogens of the Gastrointestinal System. *Lab.* Med., 22: 173-78.

Coutran, R. S. *et al.* 1989. *Robbins Pathologic Basis of Disease,* 4th ed. Philadelphia: Saunders.

Cuny, H. 1966. *Louis Pasteur: The Man and His Theories.* P. Evans, tr. New York: Ericksson.

Darnell, J. *et al,* eds. 1990. *Molecular Cell Biology,* 2nd ed. New York: Scientific Amer. Books.

De Kruif, P. 1926. *Microbe Hunters.* New York: Harcourt.

Dimmock, N. J. and Primrose, S. B. 1987. *Introduction to Modern Virology,* 3rd ed. Boston: Blackwell.

Dobell, B., ed. 1984, Oct./Nov.. A Medical Picture of the United States: A Special Section. *Amer. Heritage.*

Dubos, R. *Pasteur and Modern Science.* T. D. Brock, ed. Madison: Sc. Tech. Orig. pub. 1960.

Duclaux, E. 1973. *Pasteur: The History of a Mind.* E. Smith and F. Hedges, trs. Metuchen, NY: Scarecrow. Reprtd. from 1920 ed.

Duesberg, P. 1988. HIV is Not the Cause of AIDS. *Science,* 241:515.

Duffy, J. 1990. *The Sanitarians: A History of American Public Health.* Urbana, IL: Illinois.

Duplaix, N. 1988, May. Fleas: The Lethal Leapers. *Nat. Geo.,* 672-94.

Ewald, F. W. 1993, Apr. The Evolution of Virulence. *Scientific Amer.,* 86 ff.

Farkas, D. H. and Crisan, D., organizers. 1992. Symposium of DNA Technology. *Lab. Med.,* 23:721-770.

Fleury, H. 1987. *Institut Pasteur.* Paris: Pasteur Ins.

Fraenkel-Conrat, H. and Kimball, P. C. 1982. *Virology.* Englewood Cliffs, NJ: Prentice Hall.

Gallo, R. C. 1986, Dec. The First Human Retrovirus. *Scientific Amer.,* 88-98.

Gallo, R. C. 1987, Jan. The AIDS Virus. *Scientific Amer.,* 47-56.

Gallo, R. C. 1989, Oct. My Life Stalking AIDS. *Discover,* 30 ff.

Gallo, R. C. 1991. *AIDS and the Human Retrovirus: A Story of Scientific Discoveries.* New York: Basic Books.

Gerster, Georg. 1986, Dec. Tsetse: Fly of the Deadly Sleep. *Nat. Geo.,* 814-37.

Girard, M. 1988. The Pasteur Institute's Contributions to the Field of Virology. *Ann. Rev. Microbiol.,* 42: 745-63.

Green, J. 1968. *Medical History for Students.* Springfield, IL: Thomas.

Grun, B., ed. 1975. *The Timetables of History: A Historical Linkage of Peoples and Events.* New York: Simon and Schuster.

Hand, D. 1985, Summer. The Making of the Polio Vaccine. *Amer. Heritage Invention and Technology,* 54-57.

Hardy, G. H. 1993. *A Mathematician's Apology.* New York: Cambridge Univ. Press. First published 1940.

Hare, R. 1970. *The Birth of Penicillin.* London: Allen and Unwin.

Hendrickson, R. 1983. *More Cunning than Man: A Social History of Rats and Man.* New York: Stein and Day.

Horne, A. 1965. *The Fall of Paris: The Siege and the Commune 1870-71.* New York: St. Martin's.

Howard, B. J. 1987 *Clinical and Pathogenic Microbiology.* St. Louis: Mosby.

Hufford, D. C. 1988. A Minor Modification by R. J. Petri. *Lab. Med.,* 19: 169-70.

Hufford, D. C. 1991. Extinguishing the Invisible Fire: The Eradication of Smallpox. *Lab. Med.,* 22:27-39.

Institut Pasteur. 1987-1992. *Rapport d'activite des departments de recherche en 1987-1992.* Paris: Pasteur Institute.

Jacob, F. 1988. *The Statue Within: An Autobiography.* Franklin Philip, tr. New York: Basic Books. Orig. pub. in French, 1987.

Jacob, F. and Monod, J. 1961. Genetic Regulatory Mechanisms in the Synthesis of Proteins. *J. Mol. Biol.,* 3:318-56.

Jaret, P. 1991, Jan. The Disease Detectives. *Nat. Geo.,* 114-40.

Jaroff, L. 1988, May 23. Stop that Germ! *Time,* 56-63.

Jaroff, L. 1993, Mar. 5. Happy Birthday, Double Helix. *Time,* 56-59.

Langone, J. 1990, Dec. Emerging Viruses. *Discover,* 63-68.

Latour, B. 1988. *The Pasteurization of France,* A. Sheridan and J. Low, trs. Cambridge, MA: Harvard. Orig. pub. in French, 1984.

Lehrer, S. 1979. *Explorers of the Body.* Garden City: Doubleday.

Lennette, E. H., ed. 1980. *Manual of Clinical Microbiology.* Washington, D.C.: Amer. Sac. Microbiol.

Levine, A. J. 1992. *Viruses.* New York: Scientific Amer. Library.

Lwoff, A. and Ullman, E., eds. 1979 *Origins of Molecular Biology: A Tribute to Jacques Monod.* New York; Academic Press .

Lyons, A. S. and Petrucelli, R. J., II. 1978. *Medicine: An Illustrated History.* New York: Abrams.

Macfarlane, G. 1984. *Alexander Fleming: The Man and the Myth.* Cambridge, MA: Harvard.

Marks, G. and Beatty, W. K. 1976. *Epidemics.* New York: Scribner.

Marwick, C. 1987. Cooler Heads (of State) Prevail . . . Voilà, French-American HIV Test Accord. *J. Amer. Med. Assoc.,* 258:3482-87.

McGrew, R. E. 1985. *Encyclopedia of Medical History.* London: Macmillan.

McNeill, W. E. 1976. *Plagues and People.* Garden City, NY: Anchor.

Metchnikoff, 0. 1921. *Life of Elie Metchnikoff 1845-1916.* Boston: Houghton Mifflin. Orig. pub. in French, 1913.

Monod, J. 1971. *Chance and Necessity: An Essay of the Natural Philosophy of Modern Biology.* New York: Knopf.

Morse, S. S. and Brown, R. D. 1993. *Emerging Viruses.* New York: Oxford Univ, Press.

Nicolle, C. 1932. *Biologie de l'invention.* Paris: Librairie Felix Alcan.

Nicolle, J. 1961. *Louis Pasteur: The Story of His Major Discoveries.* New York: Basic Books.

Pernick, M. G. 1984. *A Calculus of Suffering: Pain, Professionalism, and Anesthesia in Nineteenth-Century America.* New York: Columbia.

Popovic, M. *et al.* 1984. Detection, Isolation, and Continuous Production of Cytopathic Retrovirus (HTLV-III) from Patients with AIDS and Pre-AIDS. *Science,* 224:417-500.

Popovic, M. *et al.* 1984. Frequent Detection and Isolation of Cytopathic Retroviruses (HTLV-III) from Patients with AIDS and at Risk for AIDS. *Science,* 224:500-5.

Preston, Richard. 1992, Oct 26. Crisis in the Hot Zone. *The New Yorker,* 58-81.

Robinson, Donald. 1976. *The Miracle Finders: The Stories behind the Most Important Breakthroughs in Modern Medicine.* New York: McKay.

Root-Bernstein, R. S. 1988, May-June. Setting the Stage for Discovery. *The Sciences,* 26-34.

Rosen, G. 1958. *A History of Public Health.* New York: MD Pubs.

Rosenberg, C. E. 1962. *The Cholera Years: The United States in 1832, 1849, and 1866.* Chicago: Chicago. Paperback in 1987.

Ross, R. 1989. Institut Pasteur Begins its Second Century. *Jour. Amer. Med. Assoc.,* 259:17-72.

Ryan, Frank. 1992, 1993. *The Forgotten Plague: How the Battle Against Tuberculosis was Won – and Lost.* Boston: Little, Brown.

Salomon-Bayet, C. et al. 1986 *Pasteur et la revolution Pastorienne.* Paris: Payot.

Scientific American, Special issue. 1993, Sept. Life, Death and the Immune System.

Sher, P., ed. 1988. Symposium: The Practice of Real-Time Diagnostic Microbiology. *Lab. Med.,* 19:286-321.

Stewart, Doug. 1991, Jan. These Germs Work Wonders. *Reader's Digest,* 83-86.

Stryer, L. 1988. *Biochemistry,* 3rd ed. New York: W. H. Freeman.

Sulzberger, C. L. 1966. *The American Heritage Picture History of World War II.* New York: American Heritage Pub.

Vallery-Radot, R. 1923. *The Life of Pasteur.* Mrs. R. L. Devonshire, tr. Garden City, NY: Doubleday, Page.

Ware, Jean and Hunt, Hugh. 1979. *The Several Lives of a Victorian Vet.* New York: St. Martin's.

Watson, J. 1968. *The Double Helix: A Personal Account of the Discovery of DNA.* New York: Atheneum.

Williams, G. 1987. *The Age of Miracles: Medicine and Surgery in the Nineteenth Century.* Chicago: Acad. Chi.

Woodham-Smith, C. 1962. *The Great Hunger: Ireland 1845-1849.* New York: Harper and Row.

Zureri P. 1992, Sep. 21. U.S. Refuses to Yield Royalties on AIDS Tests. *Chem. and Eng. News.,* 5.

GLOSSARY

Agar-agar – obtained from seaweed and used to solidify culture media.

Allergic – related to exaggerated specific susceptibility to a substance that is generally harmless.

Amino acid – organic acid containing an amine group.

Anaerobic – living or active in the absence of free oxygen.

Analog – a chemical substance of similar but not identical structure.

Antibiotic – a substance produced by a microorganism and capable of destroying or inhibiting the growth of other microorganisms.

Antihistamine – used to treat allergic reactions by inactivating histamine, the chemical involved in producing the inflammatory condition.

Antivivisectionist – one opposed to experimentation upon a living animal.

Aspirator – an apparatus that moves fluid by suction.

Attenuation – process of making weaker.

Autoclave – used to sterilize objects by means of superheated steam under pressure.

Biopsy – small representative piece of a lesion removed from a living subject. It is processed for microscopic examination.

Biotechnology – industrial application of biological advances.

Carcinogen – cancer producing agent.

Catalyst – accelerates a reaction without itself being changed by the reaction.

Cathode ray – projects from the cathode of a vacuum tube and consists of electrons moving in straight lines unless deflected by the action of a magnetic or electric field.

Causative organism – cause of a specific disease.

Central nervous system (CNS) – the brain and spinal cord.

Chemotherapy – the prevention or treatment of disease by use of chemical agents. The term is most frequently used with regard to malignant disease, but applies also to infectious disease.

Clone – asexually produced progeny of an individual unit; exemplified by the budding of yeast of fission of bacteria,

Clostridium tetani – spore-bearing bacillus that causes tetanus (lockjaw).

Collagen – fibrous protein of connective tissue that forms the framework of all organs in the body.

Control – a standard of comparison used in research, (Suppose 60 identical mice are suffering from disease X. Thirty are injected with drug A; 30 receive no treatment. The untreated group serves as a control for evaluating whether or not drug A is effective in treating disease X.)

Corynebacterium diphtheriae – the causative organism of diphtheria.

Cryptococcus – a fungus.

Cutaneous – pertaining to the skin.

Cystic fibrosis – an inherited disease of many of the glands with ducts.

Deltoid – muscle of upper, outer part of arm.

De novo – new.

Dextro – right.

Electrolyte – substance that forms ions in solution. Examples are $NaHCO_3$, KCl.

Electromagnetic waves – include wavelengths from short gamma rays to long radio waves that constitute the electromagnetic spectrum of light.

Electron – the negatively charged constituent of an atom.

Empirical – the pursuit of knowledge by observation and experiment.

Encephalitis – inflammation of the brain, especially due to infectious agents or their toxins.

Endocrinology – the study of hormones.

Entomology – the study of insects.

Enzootic – a local occurrence of disease among animals; comparable to endemic for humans.

Enzyme – a specific protein catalyst. Almost all currently known enzymes are proteins. Some RNA molecules have enzyme activity.

Epizootic – epidemic among animals.

Erysipelas – an acute skin infection caused by a streptococcus.

Etiology – investigation of the cause(s) of a disease.

Filtrate – material that passes through a filter. A bacterial filter does not hold back viruses.

Flora (bacteriological) – the organisms that inhabit the normal gastro-intestinal tract, vagina, skin, etc.

Gangrene – local death of soft tissues.

Gastric juice – the digestive juice secreted by cells of the stomach; it contains hydrochloric acid.

Genetic engineering – a technological advance that isolates a given gene, then clones it in an appropriate vector (e.g., bacterium or virus) to produce desired product.

Genome – the totality of genes possessed by an organism.

Hemiplegia – paralysis of one side of the body.

Hemoglobin – the oxygen-carrying protein of the red blood cell; it contains iron.

Hemolytic – a process that liberates hemoglobin from the red cell.

Hemophilia – a hereditary blood disease characterized by excessive bleeding.

Herbivorous – plant eating.

Hermetic – airtight.

Hormone – a chemical messenger formed in one organ of the body and carried to another part, where it has a regulatory action.

Hypothesis – an assumption made to test data or to guide scientific investigation.

Immunity – resistance to disease.

Infusion – a solution prepared by steeping.

In vitro – in test tube (in contrast to in *vivo* = living).

Latin Quarter (Paris) – historically the preserve of university students.

Lesion – an abnormal change in structure of an organ or part due to disease or injury.

Lipid – fats and substances such as cholesterol with similar solubility characteristics.

Medium (growth) – a nutrient system for the artificial cultivation of organisms.

Meningoencephalitis – inflammation of the brain and the membranes that cover it.

Microbiology – deals with microscopic form of life.

Micrometer – a unit of the metric system. One meter is roughly equal to 39 inches. One micrometer = one millionth meter. One nanometer = one billionth meter. One picometer = one trillionth meter.

Microorganism – an organism so small that a microscope is required to see it.

Mitosis – the process of cell division whereby a body cell divides to form two daughter cells, each with a full set of chromosomes. To be distinguished from meiosis, in which a sperm or egg cell is produced, each with half a full set.

Molecular biology – deals with the ultimate physicochemical organization of living matter.

Molecular hybridization – identification technique based on using a nucleic acid sequence ("probe") that is complementary to a sequence in the DNA or RNA of the organism to be detected.

Molecule – a unit of matter, the smallest portion of a compound that retains chemical identity with the substance in the mass.

Morbidity – incidence of disease.

Morphology – the structure or form of an object.

Motile – capable of movement.

Mucous membrane – the lining of the digestive, respiratory and genitourinary tracts.

Muscle – Skeletal muscles (biceps) are voluntary; smooth muscle (heart) is involuntary.

Mutation – a change in inherited characters. It often involves one or very few base pairs of DNA; the altered composition is reproduced in subsequent generations.

Mycobacteria – examples are the bacilli causing either tuberculosis or leprosy.

Mycology – the study of fungi.

Mycoplasma – very small bacteria that lack a cell wall.

Neonate – a newborn.

Neutrophil – a type of phagocytic white blood cell formed in the bone marrow.

Nucleoside – the combination of a nitrogenous base (usually A,T,G,C or U) with ribose or deoxyribose.

Open city – one that is completely demilitarized and left open to occupation because of its historic treasures, etc.

Oral – pertaining to the mouth.

Pandemic – an epidemic occurring throughout a large area.

Pathogen – a disease-producing microorganism.

Peritonitis – an inflammation of the membrane that lines the abdominal walls and invests the contained organs.

Peripheral – outward part.

Pertussis – whooping cough.

Plasma (blood) – the fluid remaining after blood cells have been removed from unclotted blood.

Plasmid – a mobile accessory chromosome. A bacterial cell may have none or as many as 20.

Plasmodium – a genus of Protozoa. Some cause malaria in man.

Polarimeter – measures the rotation of polarized light.

Polymerase – an enzyme that catalyzes formation of a polymer, a product made of repetitive units.

Polysaccharide – a polymer composed of carbohydrate molecules.

Prophylactic – preventing of disease.

Protein – a polymer of amino acids (these contains carbon, hydrogen, nitrogen, oxygen and sometimes sulfur); essential constituent of all cells and also of the diet of animal organisms.

Pupa (chrysalis or cocoon) – The order of metamorphosis of the silkworm is egg, larva (worm like), pupa (an inactive form), moth (sexually mature form).

Putrefaction – decomposition of organic matter.

Pyemia – blood poisoning caused by a microorganism.

Radioactivity – emission of radiant energy and particles produced by the disintegration of an atomic nucleus.

Regimen – a schedule of systematic regulation.

Rector – the head of a university or school.

Rodent – an order of gnawing mammals (rats, mice, squirrels, etc.)

Rubella – German measles.

S – symbol for the element sulfur.

Sarcoma – a cancer that originates in connective tissue.

Sepsis – a toxic condition resulting from pathogen multiplication. (When present in the blood stream, septicemia results.)

Septicemia – caused by presence in the blood of pathogenic bacteria and their associated toxins in the blood.

Sericulture – the production of raw silk by raising silkworms.

Seratherapy – a treatment of disease by the injection of immune blood serum.

Serum (plural form = sera) – the fluid, noncellular component of clotted blood.

Somatic – refers to body. Somatic cells have full sets of chromosomes, in contrast to germ cells, which have ½ the somatic number (one for each chromosome pair).

Sorbonne – world-famous college, part of the University of Paris; opened in 1253.

Specificity – condition of being peculiar to a particular individual or group.

Spore – a reproductive or resistant resting body that is often adapted to survive unfavorable conditions and to produce a new vegetative individual.

Sporozoa – subphylum of the Protozoa. Includes the causative organisms of malaria and other diseases. Some are non-pathogenic.

Staphylococcus aureus – the organism that causes boils, septicemia, osteomyelitis, etc.

Stereochemistry – deals with the spatial arrangement of atoms or groups in molecules.

Sterile – free from living organisms, especially microorganisms.

Streptococcus pyogenes – an organism that causes septicemia and other serious conditions.

Suppuration – formation of, conversion into, or act of discharging pus.

Syndrome – a group of symptoms that together characterize a disorder.

Synthesis (chemistry) – the production of a compound.

Systemic – pertaining to or affecting the body as a whole (as opposed to local).

Tabanid – refers to genus *Tabanidae*, to which belong houseflies and deer flies, whose females suck blood.

Transcription – the formation of a copy. More specifically applied to RNA synthesis complementary to a DNA precursor.

Trephine – to cut the skull.

Trypanosome – genus of Protozoa. Some trypanosomes cause African sleeping sickness.

Uranium – heavy, naturally occurring radioactive element.

Vector – a transmitting agent.

Vertebrate – an animal with a backbone.

Vesicle – a small sac involved in the secretory process of the cell.

Vibrio cholerae – "comma" bacillus that causes cholera.

Virulence – the capacity to produce disease.

White blood cell – includes neutrophil, monocyte and lymphocyte of blood, in contrast to red blood cell, which contains hemoglobin.

X-ray diffraction – a method whereby the atomic arrangement and measurements of a crystalline substance are obtained.

INDEX